RENAISSANCE THOUGHT

The Classic, Scholastic, and Humanist Strains

A revised and enlarged edition of
"The Classics and Renaissance Thought"

by

PAUL OSKAR KRISTELLER

HARPER TORCHBOOKS / **The Academy Library**
Harper & Row, Publishers
New York

TO MY COLLEAGUES
AT COLUMBIA UNIVERSITY

HARPER TORCHBOOKS / *The Academy Library*

Advisory Editor in the Humanities and Social Sciences: Benjamin Nelson

First HARPER TORCHBOOK edition published 1961

RENAISSANCE THOUGHT

hαrper ✦ τorchbooks

A reference-list of Harper Torchbooks, classified
by subjects, is printed at the end of this volume.

CONTENTS

CONTENTS

PREFACE TO THE TORCHBOOK EDITION

The invitation to have my little book, *The Classics and Renaissance Thought,* reissued in the Harper Torchbook series was certainly flattering and attractive to me, and it confirmed in a way the friendly reception given to this book by many readers and critics. I also appreciate the opportunity to add two essays not contained in the original edition, and to make a number of small corrections and additions, especially in the footnotes and bibliography. At the same time, I am keenly aware of many shortcomings which I could not remove without writing another book, or even not eliminate at all. The subject which I am trying to discuss is very large indeed, and a vast amount of studies have been written about some of its aspects whereas others have remained more or less unexplored. It is obviously impossible for a single scholar to master such a subject. Moreover, many problems on which I touch have been a matter of much controversy among historians, and although I am aware of many different opinions of greater or lesser merit, I obviously have no choice but to express my own, without being able to present in a short and modestly annotated book the evidence on which this opinion rests. Yet it is this evidence which really counts in giving strength to any historical opinion, and not the eloquence with which it is expressed, or the degree to which it fits certain cherished or fashionable interests or preferences of the moment. I should like to warn especially the students and other younger persons who may happen to read this book against the widespread habit of arguing about historical opinions, without looking for the documentary basis which supports them, and of playing one scholarly authority against another. I do not recognize the authority of any scholar beyond the testimony of historical reality, and I should be untrue to my own principles if

I were to claim any such authority for myself. Finally, the very attempt to treat a large and complicated topic in a short synthesis forces the writer to simplify, and to omit qualifications, and everything he says is at best an approximation. I should like to hope that at least some of my readers will use this book as a starting point for reading some of the literary, scholarly or philosophical works of the Renaissance period, and thus judge for themselves where I am right, and where I fail.

I should like to explain that the original book reproduced the Martin Classical Lectures which I had been invited to deliver at Oberlin College in 1954. The fact that these lectures were delivered under the auspices of a Department of Classics, and published in a series devoted to classical studies, accounts for the special and limited point of view from which Renaissance thought is discussed in this book. I considered it as my main task to show the impact and influence of classical studies and of ancient sources upon the philosophical and general thought of the Renaissance period. I did not mean to deny, even by implication, that Renaissance thought was also indebted to medieval influences, or that it formulated many original ideas of its own. These aspects, though as important as, or even more important than, the one I treat, merely did not fall within the scope of my presentation. These limitations will be removed, at least to some extent, in this new edition since it will add two other papers or chapters not contained in the original edition. The paper on "Humanism and Scholasticism in the Italian Renaissance" will emphasize, at least in a formal and institutional sense, the medieval antecedents of Renaissance humanism and Aristotelianism, and will at the same time supply some of the historical documentation on which the first two chapters of the original book were based. The paper on "The Philosophy of Man in the Italian Renaissance" will give an example of some actual ideas expressed by Renaissance thinkers, focusing primarily, but not exclusively, on the Renaissance Platonists, and showing how they transformed their admired classical sources and incorporated them into their own novel modes of thought.

I should like to thank all those who have made this new edition possible: the publishing house of Harper & Brothers for their interest and initiative in assuming its publication; Oberlin College and the Harvard University Press for their permission to have the book republished in a somewhat altered form; Edizioni di Storia e Letteratura in Rome for their willingness to have the two added papers republished from my volume, *Studies in Renaissance Thought and Letters,* in which they appeared in 1956. I also wish to thank those friends and fellow scholars who through reviews or letters or in personal conversation pointed out to me some of my errors, and must ask them to forgive me if this new edition in which I have been able to make but a few changes should fail to correct all of them. Among these friendly critics, I should like to mention especially Ludwig Bieler (Dublin), R. R. Bolgar (Cambridge), Douglas Bush (Harvard), James Hutton (Cornell), Otis Green (University of Pennsylvania), William Hay (University of Wisconsin), Raymond Lebègue (Paris), N. Orsini (University of Wisconsin), Alexander Turyn (University of Illinois), and Edward Williamson (Wesleyan University).

Columbia University
January 15, 1961

PAUL OSKAR KRISTELLER

PREFACE TO THE ORIGINAL EDITION

I WISH to express my thanks and appreciation to my colleagues at Oberlin College who kindly invited me to deliver these lectures (originally published as *The Classics and Renaissance Thought,* Chs. 1-4 below) on February 22-26, 1954, and decided afterwards to have them published. I welcomed the opportunity thus offered me to present my views on a subject which has attracted me for many years and which, to my knowledge, has not been treated in any recent comprehensive study. I also feel somewhat hesitant to publish these views since I cannot prove or document them in such a short study, and since I happen to disagree with many distinguished scholars whose work I have yet every reason to respect.

The lectures are published here essentially as delivered, but I was kindly allowed to add a section of notes. I decided to use this space mainly to acquaint the more curious reader with those studies in which he may find further detail and evidence relevant to the various aspects of our subject.

To those of my readers who are primarily interested in philosophy and its history, I must apologize for the scarcity of doctrinal analysis. Within the limited time and space at my disposal, I felt that I would do more justice to my subject by trying to draw a rough but comprehensive map of Renaissance learning in some of its aspects, and thus to help prepare a system of orientation in which each thinker and each philosophical idea might eventually be assigned their proper historical place.

PAUL OSKAR KRISTELLER

Columbia University
August 13, 1954.

RENAISSANCE
THOUGHT

1. THE HUMANIST MOVEMENT

I GREATLY appreciate the honor of being invited to deliver the Martin Classical Lectures this year, and of being a guest of Oberlin College, an institution noted for its distinguished tradition in the humanities, and well known to Renaissance scholars for the outstanding work of its former president, Ernest Wilkins. Ever since I myself received a training in classical philology and wrote my doctoral dissertation on a Greek philosopher, I have retained, in the face of the changing winds of fashionable opinion, a firm belief in the continuing value of classical studies and of a classical education. Thus I have never failed, in my efforts to understand certain philosophical writers of the Renaissance period, to pay due attention to the influences exercised upon them by classical antiquity, and I greatly welcome this opportunity to present in a more comprehensive manner my views on this important subject, as fully as the available time and the state of my information will permit.

Since philosophical and historical no less than political discussions are apt to sink into confusion through the use of vague and ill-defined notions, and since I feel unable to speak about my subject without using some of the general terms traditionally applied to it, I should like to explain first how I plan to use some of these terms.

The meaning of the term "Renaissance" has been the subject of an unending controversy among recent historians, who have been debating about the value, the distinctive characteristics, the time limits, and the very existence of that historical period.[1] I shall not repeat or refute any of the arguments proposed by others, but merely state that by "the Renaissance" I understand that period of Western European history which extends approximately from 1300 to 1600, without any preconception as to the characteristics or merits of that period, or of those periods preceding and following it. I do not pretend to assert that there was a sharp break at the beginning or end of "the Renaissance," or to deny that there was a good deal of continuity. I should even admit that in some respects the changes which occurred in the twelfth and thirteenth or in the seventeenth and eighteenth centuries were more profound than the changes of the fourteenth and fifteenth. I merely maintain that the so-called Renaissance period has a distinctive physiognomy of its own, and that the inability of historians to find a simple and satisfactory definition for it does not entitle us to doubt its existence; otherwise, by the same token, we should have to question the existence of the Middle Ages, or of the eighteenth century. The Renaissance is a very complex period and it encompassed, just as do the Middle Ages or any other period, a good many chronological, regional, and social differences. Not being able to do equal justice to all aspects of the Renaissance, I shall focus our attention, though not exclusively, upon Italy in the fifteenth and early sixteenth centuries. Whereas the cultural differences between Italy and Northern Europe were no less marked during the high Middle Ages than during the Renaissance, in the fifteenth century Italy, along with the Low Countries, attained a position of intellectual leadership in Western Europe which she had not possessed in the preceding age. If Europe during the Middle Ages had one or several Renaissances, as some scholars believe, Italy's share in these earlier "Renaissances" was rather limited. On the other hand, if the Renaissance of the fifteenth century, seen against the background of the French Middle Ages, does not appear to some historians like a rebirth of Europe, it certainly appeared to its contemporaries, against the background of the Italian Middle Ages, like a rebirth of Italy. Moreover, I shall not discuss the Renaissance in terms of a few outstanding and well-known thinkers and writers alone, but I shall rather try to draw a cultural map of the period, taking into account the vast amount of information hidden away in the bibliographies of early editions, in the collections and catalogues of manuscript books, and in the records of schools, universities, and other learned institutions. This approach will enable us also to view the great writers of the period in a better perspective, and to judge in each case whether we are dealing with the representative expression of a broad trend of thinking, or with the isolated and original contribution of an individual mind.

If we try to understand the thought and philosophy of the Renaissance, or of any other period, we are of course confronted with a variety of currents and of individual writers, which defies any attempt at a general description. The task becomes even more complex if we extend our view beyond the area of "philosophy" in the narrow and technical sense, characterized by professional traditions and the discipline of method, into the vast field of general thought embodied in the writings of poets and prose authors, of scholars, scientists, or theologians. To some extent the historian of philosophy is driven to follow this course, since the very meaning of philosophy, the emphasis it puts on certain problems, its relations to other fields of intellectual endeavor, the place it occupies in the system of culture, are apt to undergo a continuous change. On the other hand, our task is simplified in so far as we are not considering Renaissance thought in its originality or in its entire content, but merely in its relation to classical antiquity.

This relation in turn calls for one further preliminary remark. To be sure, the world of classical antiquity, and especially its literature and philosophy, seems to possess a solid reality which, like a high mountain range, has remained above the horizon for many centuries. Yet on closer inspection, it becomes apparent that the use made of this heritage by later generations has been subject to many changes. Each period has offered a different selection and interpretation of ancient literature, and individual Greek and Latin authors as well as their individual writings have seen more or less deep ebbs and tides of popularity at different times. Hence we shall not be surprised to learn that the Renaissance attitude towards classical antiquity differed in many ways from that of medieval or modern times. Modern classicism, which originated in the eighteenth century and continues to influence our approach to the classics, though it has been modified since then by various currents of historical, archaeological, and anthropological scholarship, has tended to focus our attention upon the literature and thought of the early and classical Greek period down to the fourth century B.C., and to a lesser degree upon Roman literature to the first century A.D.; whereas the later phases of Greek and Latin literature, and especially of its doctrinal and scientific literature, have been comparatively neglected. Medieval Europe, on the other hand, lived for many centuries in the direct tradition of Roman antiquity, used the Latin language as a medium for its learning and much of its literature and business, and knew some though not all of the ancient Roman poets and prose authors quite thoroughly, yet was with a few exceptions unfamiliar with the Greek language and with its classical literature. Moreover, the early Middle Ages, from the time of the Latin Church Fathers, were concerned with the problem of reconciling the study of the pagan classics with the teachings and commands of Christianity, a problem which received added urgency from the fact that the learning of the period was almost entirely in the possession of the Catholic clergy. During the later Middle Ages, and more specifically between the middle of the eleventh and the end of the thirteenth centuries, profound changes occurred in the intellectual culture of Western Europe. A growing professional interest developed in philosophy and in the sciences, which was kindled by Arabic influences and nourished by a flood of Latin translations, from the Arabic and from the Greek, through which many writings of Aristotle and of a few other Greek philosophers, of Euclid and Ptolemy, Galen and Hippocrates became for the first time available to Western students. This later medieval interest in the works of certain Greek philosophers and scientists must be clearly distinguished from the earlier medieval study of the classical Latin poets and prose writers. Actually, there was a conflict between the representatives of the *artes*, that is, of the liberal arts and the scientific and philosophical disciplines, and the followers of the *authores*, that is, of the great books, and by the thirteenth century the latter tendency had suffered a decisive, though perhaps temporary, defeat.[2] The Renaissance attitude towards the classics inherited some features from the Middle Ages, but was different from the earlier and later medieval approach, as well as from that of modern classicism. Renaissance scholars continued or resumed the study of the Latin authors that had been cultivated by the medieval grammarians, but greatly expanded and improved it, and also pursued it for its own sake. They were not anti-Christian, but as laymen they did not subordinate the development of secular learning to its amalgamation with religious or theological doctrine. Moreover, they added the study of the Greek language and of its entire literature, going far beyond the limits of science and of Aristotelian philosophy. Finally, guided by their enthusiasm for everything ancient, and by the conscious program of imitating and reviving ancient learning and literature, Renaissance scholars had a much more comprehensive interest in ancient literature than either medieval or modern students. They did not despise late or minor authors, in spite of a widespread preference for Cicero or Vergil, and even accepted many apocryphal works as authentic. As a result of this broad interest, classical studies occupied in the Renaissance a more central place in the civilization of the period, and were more intimately linked with its other intellectual tendencies and achievements, than at any earlier or later time in the history of Western Europe.

If we are to understand the role of classical studies in the Renaissance, we must begin with the humanist movement. The term "Humanism" has been associated with the Renaissance and its classical studies for more than a hundred years, but in recent times it has become the source of much philosophical and historical confusion. In present discourse, almost any kind of concern with human values is called "humanistic," and consequently a great variety of thinkers, religious or antireligious, scientific or antiscientific, lay claim to what has become a rather elusive label of praise. We might ignore this twentieth-century confusion, but for the direct impact it has had upon historical studies. For many historians, knowing that the term "humanism" has been traditionally associated with the Renaissance, and seeing that some features of the modern notion of "humanism" seem to have their counterparts in the thought of that period, have cheerfully applied the term "humanism" in its vague modern meaning to the Renaissance and to other periods of the past, speaking of Renaissance humanism, medieval humanism, or Christian humanism, in a fashion which defies any definition and seems to have little or nothing left of the basic classicist meaning of Renaissance humanism.[3] This seems to me a bad example of that widespread tendency among historians to impose the terms and labels of our modern time upon the thought of the past. If we want to understand the philosophy of the Renaissance or of any other period, we must try not only to separate the interpretation of the authentic thought of the period from the evaluation and critique of its merits, but also to recapture the original meaning in which that period employed certain categories and classifications which either have become unfamiliar to us, or have acquired different connotations. In the case of the term "Humanism," its historical ancestry has become pretty clear as a result of recent studies. The term *Humanismus* was coined in 1808 by the German educator, F. J. Niethammer, to express the emphasis on the Greek and Latin classics in secondary education, as against the rising demands for a more practical and more scientific training.[4] In this sense, the word was applied by many historians of the nineteenth century to the scholars of the Renaissance, who had also advocated and established the central role of the classics in the curriculum, and who in some German cities had founded in the sixteenth century the same schools which were still carrying on that tradition in the nineteenth. The term *Humanismus,* in the specific sense of a program and ideal of classical education, cannot be dismissed on account of its comparatively recent origin. For it is derived from another similar word, "humanist," whose origin can be traced back to the Renaissance itself. *Humanista* in Latin, and its vernacular equivalents in Italian, French, English, and other languages, were terms commonly used in the sixteenth century for the professor or teacher or student of the humanities, and this usage remained alive and was well understood until the eighteenth century.[5] The word, to judge from its earliest appearance known so far, seems to have originated in the student slang of the Italian universities, where the professor of the humanities came to be called *umanista,* after the analogy of his colleagues in the older disciplines, to whom the terms *legista, jurista, canonista,* and *artista* had been applied for several centuries. The term *humanista,* coined at the height of the Renaissance period, was in turn derived from an older term, that is, from the "humanities" or *studia humanitatis.* This term was apparently used in the general sense of a liberal or literary education by such ancient Roman authors as Cicero and Gellius, and this use was resumed by the Italian scholars of the late fourteenth century.[6] By the first half of the fifteenth cen-

tury, the *studia humanitatis* came to stand for a clearly defined cycle of scholarly disciplines, namely grammar, rhetoric, history, poetry, and moral philosophy,[7] and the study
of each of these subjects was understood to include the reading and interpretation of its standard ancient writers in
Latin and, to a lesser extent, in Greek. This meaning of the
studia humanitatis remained in general use through the sixteenth century and later, and we may still find an echo of it
in our use of the term "humanities." Thus Renaissance
humanism was not as such a philosophical tendency or system, but rather a cultural and educational program which
emphasized and developed an important but limited area of
studies. This area had for its center a group of subjects that
was concerned essentially neither with the classics nor with
philosophy, but might be roughly described as literature. It
was to this peculiar literary preoccupation that the very in-
tensive and extensive study which the humanists devoted to
the Greek and especially to the Latin classics owed its peculiar character, which differentiates it from that of modern
classical scholars since the second half of the eighteenth century. Moreover, the *studia humanitatis* includes one philosophical discipline, that is, morals, but it excludes by definition such fields as logic, natural philosophy, and metaphysics,
as well as mathematics and astronomy, medicine, law, and
theology, to mention only such fields as had a firmly established place in the university curriculum and in the classifi-
cation schemes of the period. This stubborn fact seems to
me to provide irrefutable evidence against the repeated attempts to identify Renaissance humanism with the philosophy, the science, or the learning of the period as a whole.[8]
On the other hand, if we want to apply the Renaissance term
"humanist" to the medieval period, which did not use it, we
may choose to call "humanists" certain Carolingian scholars
such as Alcuin or Lupus of Ferrières, or certain twelfth-cen-
tury authors such as John of Salisbury or the grammarians

of Orléans and Chartres, on account of the affinity of their learned interests with those of the Italian humanists of the Renaissance. But if we call St. Thomas Aquinas a "humanist" because of his indebtedness to the Greek philosopher Aristotle, we might as well apply the same label to all other Aristotelian philosophers of the later Middle Ages, and also to all medieval mathematicians, astronomers, medical authors, or jurists, on account of their dependence upon such ancient authorities as Euclid, Ptolemy, Galen, or the Corpus Juris; and thus we shall have deprived ourselves of a very helpful distinction indeed. Hence I should like to ask you to keep the Renaissance meaning of "humanities" and "humanist" well in mind whenever I use the term "humanism" in these lectures, and to forget our modern uses of the word as completely as you can. If you fail to do so, I cannot be held responsible for the resulting confusion.

The central importance of literary preoccupations in Renaissance humanism might be illustrated by the professional status of the humanists, most of whom were active either as teachers of the humanities in secondary schools or universities, or as secretaries to princes or cities, and by the bulk of their extant writings, which consists of orations, letters, poems, and historical works and which is in part still unpublished or even unsifted. It cannot be our task in this lecture to give an account of these professional activities of the humanists, or of their contributions to Neolatin literature and to the various vernacular literatures. I merely want to point out that Renaissance humanism must be understood as a characteristic phase in what may be called the rhetorical tradition in Western culture. This tradition is as old as the Greek Sophists, and it is very much alive in our own day, although the word "rhetoric" has become distasteful to many people. For the studies of speech and composition, of English and creative writing, of advertisement and business correspondence are nothing but modern varieties of the age-old rhetorical enterprise that tries to teach oral and written expression by means of rules and models. Since the rhetorician offers to speak and to write about everything, and the philosopher tries to think about everything, they have always been rivals in their claim to provide a universal training of the mind. This rivalry appeared in Plato's polemic against the Sophists; it continued throughout the later centuries of Greek antiquity in the competing schools of the philosophers and of the rhetoricians,[9] it was largely forgotten among the Romans and their successors in the early Middle Ages, for the simple reason that they had a strong rhetorical, but no philosophical, tradition; it reappeared in various ways in the high Middle Ages with the rise of philosophical studies,[10] and again in the Renaissance when humanistic learning began to compete with the scholastic tradition of Aristotelian philosophy. The relation between the two traditions has been complicated by the fact that the rhetoricians ever since Isocrates have been concerned with morals and have liked to call themselves philosophers, whereas the philosophers ever since Aristotle have tended to offer their own version of rhetoric as a part of philosophy. The historical significance of rhetoric cannot be fully understood unless we take into consideration not only the rhetorical theories of philosophers such as Aristotle and his scholastic successors, or of rhetoricians who tried to combine rhetoric and philosophy such as Cicero, but also the rhetoric of the rhetoricians, that is, of the authors professionally concerned with the practice of speaking and writing. In medieval Italy, this profession was strongly represented from the late eleventh century on by the so-called *dictatores* who taught and practiced, on the basis of textbooks and models, the eminently practical art of composing documents, letters, and public speeches.[11] It has become clear as a result of recent investigation that the humanists of the Renaissance were the professional successors of the medieval Italian *dictatores*, and inherited from them the various patterns of epistolography and public oratory, all more or less determined by the customs and practical needs of later medieval society. Yet the medieval *dictatores* were no classical scholars and used no classical models for their compositions. It was the novel contribution of the humanists to add the firm belief that in order to write and to speak well it was necessary to study and to imitate the ancients. Thus we can understand why classical studies in the Renaissance were rarely, if ever, separated from the literary and practical aim of the rhetorician to write and to speak well. This practical and professional connection provided a strong incentive towards classical studies and helped to supply for them the necessary manpower for their proper development. For I cannot help feeling that the achievements of a given nation or period in particular branches of culture depend not only on individual talents, but also on the available professional channels and tasks into which these talents can be drawn and for which they are trained. This is a subject to which cultural and social historians apparently have not yet paid sufficient attention.

If we try to survey the contributions of the Renaissance humanists to classical scholarship, it will be helpful to distinguish between the Latin and the Greek fields. In the field of Latin studies, there was a much closer connection with the rhetorical and practical interests just mentioned, and also with the scholarly traditions of the Middle Ages, although we should keep in mind that these traditions had been less cultivated in Italy, the cradle of Renaissance humanism, than in the Northern countries, and had suffered a decline even in France during the period immediately preceding the Renaissance. Most attention has been paid to the humanist discoveries of classical Latin authors unknown or neglected during the Middle Ages.[12] The merit of these discoveries has been unduly disparaged with the remark that the manuscripts found by the humanists were written during the Middle Ages, and that the respective authors were consequently not unknown or in need of a discovery. If an ancient Latin text survived only in one or two Carolingian manuscripts, and if there are but scanty traces of its having been read during the subsequent centuries, the fact that such a text was found by a humanist and made generally available through numerous copies does constitute a discovery. On the other hand, the fact that some classical Latin authors such as Vergil or Ovid or Seneca or Boethius were widely known throughout the Middle Ages does not refute the equally obvious fact that some other authors such as Lucretius or Tacitus or Manilius were discovered by the humanists. It would be wrong to maintain that classical Latin literature as a whole was neglected during the Middle Ages, or to deny that a certain nucleus of it was commonly studied. It would be equally wrong to deny that as a result of the humanist discoveries the available patrimony of Latin literature was extended almost to its present limits, and that the writings added to the medieval nucleus included, besides less important texts, also some that have been important and influential. Moreover, the case of such a central author as Cicero shows that the dividing line between the medieval nucleus and the humanist discoveries may separate the individual works of the same writer. For whereas some of his works, such as the *De inventione* and the *De officiis,* were commonly used during the Middle Ages, his *Brutus,* his letters and many of his orations were rediscovered by the humanists. Less sensational but perhaps more effective was the tremendous activity of the humanists as copyists, and later as editors, of the Latin classics. The wide diffusion and popularity of the Latin classics in the sixteenth century and afterwards would not have been possible without the printing press. In the fourteenth and fifteenth centuries, the introduction of paper as a cheaper writing material and the organization of a regular trade in manuscript books had a similar effect, and the enormous number of manuscript copies of the Latin classics from these centuries has escaped general attention because they have been rarely used by modern editors on account of their late origin. Along with the copying and editing of the Latin authors, the humanists developed the techniques of textual and historical criticism, studied Latin orthography, grammar, and rhetoric, ancient history and mythology, as well as archaeology, epigraphy, and antiquarian subjects. Finally, the humanists produced a vast body of commentaries on the various Latin authors, which are the direct result of their teaching activity and in which they incorporated their philological and historical knowledge as well as their critical judgment. This body of literature is undoubtedly related to the commentaries on Latin authors written by medieval grammarians, but the extent of this connection remains to be investigated, and there is reason to believe that the humanist commentaries became gradually more critical and more scholarly in the course of the Renaissance period.[15a]

The humanist study of Greek was much less affected by the tradition of rhetorical practice or by Western medieval precedents. Greek books and Greek instruction were rare exceptions during the Middle Ages;[13] consequently, the work of the humanists appears much more novel when attention is focused on the Greek rather than on the Latin classics. On the other hand, the study of the Greek classics had flourished more or less continually during the medieval centuries in the Byzantine East, and Renaissance humanists in their Greek studies were clearly influenced by scholarly contacts with their Byzantine colleagues. The extent of this influence, not only on the acquisition of particular knowledge but also on the approach and attitude of Western scholars towards Greek literature, cannot yet be estimated at present.[14] As is well known, the humanists introduced Greek into the curriculum of all universities and of the better secondary schools of Western Europe, and they also imported from the Byzantine and later Turkish East, through purchase and through less honorable means, a large number of manuscripts containing almost the entire body of extant Greek literature, which was thus deposited in Western libraries and diffused through handwritten copies and printed editions. But since the knowledge of Greek was comparatively rare even during the Renaissance, whereas Latin remained the common vehicle of learning and instruction, the general diffusion of Greek literature depended no less on Latin translations than on editions of the original Greek texts. Thus it was an important, though not yet sufficiently appreciated, achievement of the Renaissance scholars that they gradually translated into Latin almost the entire body of Greek literature then known, and thus introduced it into the main stream of Western thought. Whereas comparatively few writings had been translated from Greek into Latin in ancient times, during the later Middle Ages a large body of such translations was made which covered mainly writings on mathematics, astronomy, and medicine, besides the philosophical works of Aristotle. The Renaissance humanists supplied many new versions of the same works which had been translated before, and the relative merits of these competing medieval and humanist translations have been debated with some passion, but not yet sufficiently investigated.[15] More obvious are the merits of the humanists in those numerous cases where they translated works of Greek antiquity for the first time. The catalogue of these translations cannot yet be given in the present state of our knowledge, but it appears certain that the body of newly translated material includes practically all of Greek poetry, historiography, and oratory, much of Greek patristic theology and of non-Aristotelian philosophy, and even some additional writings on the sciences of mathematics and medicine. The authors all or most of whose writings thus became known to Western readers include Homer and Sophocles, Herodotus and Thucydides, Xenophon, Isocrates, Demosthenes, Plutarch and Lucian, Epicurus, Sextus and Plotinus, to mention only a few writers of obvious merit or influence. Again, the dividing line between works translated in the Middle Ages and first translated during the Renaissance often separates the individual writings of the same author, as is the case with Plato, Hippocrates, Galen, and Ptolemy, with many Aristotelian commentators and patristic theologians, and even with Aristotle. Thus it will be apparent that both in the Latin and in the Greek fields the Middle Ages possessed a significant selection of classical sources, but that Renaissance humanism extended its knowledge almost to the entire range of its extant remains, that is to the point where modern scholarship has made its further discoveries from palimpsests and papyri.

When we try to assess the contributions of the humanists to the philosophical thought of the Renaissance, we must mention in passing the attempts at a reform of logic, due to Valla, Agricola, Ramus, and Nizolius, which were in part guided by rhetorical considerations, but represent an episode of great historical significance. Yet the most extensive and direct expression of the thought of the humanists proper must be sought in a body of their writings that we have not yet mentioned, namely their treatises and dialogues, many of which deal, as might be expected, with moral questions, including educational, political, and religious problems.[16] Most of these treatises, whether their authors are Petrarch or Salutati, Bruni or Valla, Poggio or Filelfo, Francesco Barbaro or Leone Battista Alberti, are the works of consummate writers and scholars, but must appear somewhat amateurish to a reader acquainted with the works of the greater Greek, scholastic, or modern philosophers. They often seem to lack not only originality, but also coherence, method, and substance, and if we try to sum up their arguments and conclusions, leaving aside citations, examples, and commonplaces, literary ornaments and digressions, we are frequently left with nearly empty hands. Thus I have not been convinced by the attempts to interpret these humanistic treatises as contributions to speculative thought, or to find in humanist philology the seeds of Vico's philosophy of language, although the eighteenth-century philosopher certainly inherited his erudition and his interest in history and literature from the humanists. Nevertheless the humanist treatises are important in many ways and deserve a more thorough study than they have received. They please through the elegance and clarity of their style and their vivid personal and historical flavor as well as through their well-selected and mellowed classical wisdom. They also air or express interesting opinions on matters that occupied the heart and thought of the authors and their contemporaries. They derive added importance from the fact that some of the genuine and more concrete problems of moral philosophy were apparently neglected by the professional philosophers of the time, and thus the humanists prepared the ground for a more systematic treatment of the same problems by later philosophers. This seems to be the function of poets, writers, and amateur thinkers at any time when the professional philosophers are absorbed in technicalities and refuse to discuss certain basic problems.

If we remember the range and extent of humanist scholarship and literature, we shall not be surprised to learn that Isocrates, Plutarch, and Lucian were among their favorite authors, but that the ancient writer who earned their highest admiration was Cicero. Renaissance humanism was an age of Ciceronianism in which the study and imitation of Cicero was a widespread concern, although the exaggeration of this tendency also found its critics. Cicero's influence in the Renaissance has been the subject of more than one study,[17] and we can merely try to state in a few words some of the main features of this influence. Above all, Cicero's rhetorical works provided the theory, and his orations, letters, and dialogues the concrete models for the main branches of prose literature, whereas the structure of his well-cadenced sentences was imitated in all kinds of literary compositions. Through his philosophical writings, he served as a source of information for several schools of Greek philosophy and also as a model of that eclectic type of thinking which was prepared to take its crumbs of knowledge wherever it could find them, and which also characterizes many of the humanist treatises.   Finally, the synthesis of philosophy and rhetoric in his work provided the humanists with a favorite ideal, namely the combination of eloquence and wisdom, an ideal which pervades so much of Renaissance literature.   It is true that many of the minor humanists were quite satisfied with eloquence alone, or convinced that enough wisdom would come along with it without further effort; whereas many others took shallow commonplaces for wisdom.   Yet we should also remember that many of the greater humanists such as Petrarch and Salutati, Valla and Bruni, Alberti and Pontano, Erasmus, More and Montaigne were able to add genuine wisdom to their eloquence.

After the middle of the fifteenth century, the influence of humanistic learning spread outside the limits of the *studia humanitatis* into all areas of Renaissance culture, including philosophy and the various sciences.   This was due not only to the fashionable prestige of the humanities, but also to the fact that practically every scholar received a humanistic training in secondary school before he acquired a professional training in any of the other disciplines at the university.   On the other hand, some of the humanists also began to realize that a thorough study of philosophy should be added to the *studia humanitatis*.[18]   Consequently, we find a number of important thinkers in the fifteenth century, such as Cusanus, Ficino, and Pico, and many more in the sixteenth, who combined a more or less thoroughgoing humanist background with solid philosophical achievements which were derived from different origins.[19] I believe that the discussion of Renaissance humanism in its original meaning has been confused by the attempts to claim these philosophers as an integral part of it, and thus to identify humanism with all or most of Renaissance philosophy. On the other hand, these thinkers should be taken into account if we wish to understand the indirect influence of humanism on Renaissance thought, an influence which in many ways was even more important than its direct contribution.

The pervasive influence of humanism on all aspects of Renaissance culture and especially on its philosophical thought is a vast subject of which we can mention only a few major points. Some influential aspects of Renaissance humanism are characteristic of the age, and not necessarily due to classical influences. There is the emphasis on man, on his dignity and privileged place in the universe, which was forcefully expressed by Petrarch, Manetti, and other humanists, and later elaborated or criticized by many philosophers.[20] This idea was undoubtedly implied in, and connected with, the concept and program of the *studia humanitatis,* and it has provided the opening entry for many modern interpretations of humanism, whenever the specific content of the humanities was left out of account. Another characteristic feature is the tendency to express, and to consider worth expressing, the concrete uniqueness of one's feelings, opinions, experiences, and surroundings, a tendency which appears in the biographical and descriptive literature of the time as well as in its portrait painting, which is present in all the writings of the humanists, and which finds its fullest philosophical expression in Montaigne, who claims that his own self is the main subject matter of his philosophy.[21] This tendency has been adequately described by Burckhardt, who called it "individualism," and those who have debated the individualism of the Renaissance have missed this point entirely when they understand by individualism merely the existence of great individuals, or the nominalist emphasis on the reality of particular things as against universals. Yet more relevant to our purpose are those aspects of humanist influence which are directly connected with its fundamental classicism. I am inclined to find its traces in the taste for elegance, neatness, and clarity of style and literary form which distinguishes the writings of many, if not all, Renaissance scientists and philosophers, and which is not always or entirely a mere external feature. More obvious is the ubiquity of classical sources, quotations, and ideas in Renaissance thought that were either introduced or popularized by the work of the humanists. Without impairing the originality of achievement, this classical element appears in one way or another in all areas, in the visual arts as in the various sciences. Although nearly nothing was known about ancient music, ancient musical theories were used to justify certain innovations of the time, and the humanist reform of handwriting from which our Roman characters are derived was based on the Carolingian minuscule which they mistakenly thought to be the script of the ancient Romans. Livy and Polybius affected the political thought of Machiavelli, Plato that of Thomas More, and Tacitus the theorists of the later sixteenth century. And there was no thinker in the sixteenth century who did not use, besides the traditional texts of Aristotle, Cicero, and Boethius, the newly acquired writings of Plato and the Neoplatonists, of Plutarch and Lucian, of Diogenes Laertius, of Sextus and Epictetus, or the apocryphal works attributed to the Pythagoreans, to Orpheus, Zoroaster, and Hermes Trismegistus.

One more effect of humanism upon Renaissance thought consisted in the repeated attempts to revive or restate the philosophical doctrines of particular ancient thinkers or schools, which in a sense represent the application to philosophy of the revival or renaissance of ancient learning which was one of the favorite slogans of the humanists, and from which the much-debated modern name of the period derives its origin.   Whereas the tendency of most humanists was rather eclectic, some of them, and also certain other philosophers with a humanist background, preferred a restatement of some particular ancient doctrine.   Thus we find a kind of Christianized Epicureanism in Valla; whereas the natural philosophy of Epicurus found an advocate, after the end of the Renaissance proper, in Gassendi, and even influenced some aspects of Galileo's physics.   Stoic philosophy had a wide influence on the moral thought of the Renaissance, until it found a systematic and learned interpreter towards the very end of the period in Justus Lipsius, whose writings exercised a strong influence on the moralists of the subsequent centuries.   And various brands of ancient skepticism were adopted, with some modifications, by Montaigne, Sanchez, and others before they came to influence early modern thought down to Bayle and Hume.   This tendency also supplies the broader context for at least some aspects of Renaissance Platonism, Aristotelianism, and Christianity.

Thus I should like to understand Renaissance humanism, at least in its origin and in its typical representatives, as a broad cultural and literary movement, which in its substance was not philosophical, but had important philosophical implications and consequences.   I have been unable to discover in the humanist literature any common philosophical doctrine, except a belief in the value of man and the humanities and in the revival of ancient learning.   Any particular statement gleaned from the work of a humanist may be countered by contrary assertions in the writings of contemporary authors or even of the same author.   On the other hand, the common cultural orientation and background might be combined in the case of each author with any set of philosophical or scientific or theological opinions or cognitions, and actually came to cut across all national, religious, philosophical, and even professional divisions of the period. Since the entire range of Greek philosophical and scientific literature was made more completely available to the West than it had been in the Middle Ages or in Roman antiquity, there was a large store of new ideas and notions that had to be tried out and appropriated until its lesson was finally exhausted, and it is this process of intellectual fermentation which characterizes the period and which accounts at least in part for the difference between Thomas Aquinas and Descartes. For only after this process had been completed, did seventeenth-century philosophy make its new beginning on the basis of early physical science, whereas the heritage of the Renaissance continued to feed many secondary currents of thought down to the nineteenth century.

2. THE ARISTOTELIAN TRADITION

A MONG the many philosophers of classical antiquity, two thinkers have exercised a wider and deeper influence upon posterity than any others, Plato and Aristotle. The controversy and interplay between Platonism and Aristotelianism has occupied a central place in many periods of Western thought, and even the modern student who receives but an elementary introduction to Greek philosophy will inevitably get acquainted with the thought, and with some of the writings, of Plato and of Aristotle. This overwhelming importance of Plato and Aristotle is due to two factors which are in a sense related to each other: the intrinsic greatness of their thought, and the preservation of their writings. Aside from such authors as Sextus Empiricus, Epictetus, Alexander of Aphrodisias, and the Neoplatonists, who represent the latest phases of ancient thought, Plato and Aristotle are the only important Greek philosophers whose writings have been extant, either completely or to a considerable extent. Neither their predecessors such as Heraclitus, Parmenides, or Democritus, nor their successors such as Chrysippus, Panaetius, or Posidonius have been so fortunate, and others such as Theophrastus and Epicurus have fared but slightly better.

Historians of Western thought have often expressed the view that the Renaissance was basically an age of Plato, whereas the Middle Ages had been an age of Aristotle. This view can no longer be maintained without considerable qualifications. In spite of a widespread revolt against the authority of Aristotle, the tradition of Aristotelianism continued to be very strong throughout the Renaissance period, and in some ways it even increased rather than declined. On the other hand, Platonism had its own medieval roots and precedents, and even during the Renaissance, its precise place and the extent of its influence are somewhat elusive and difficult to define, in spite of its undoubted depth and vigor. Nevertheless, Aristotle's influence in the Renaissance was clearly linked with a tradition that originated in the later Middle Ages, and Platonism was understood by its representatives and their contemporaries as a revival. These circumstances may explain why I am going to discuss Aristotle's influence before that of Plato, although Aristotle was Plato's pupil and presupposed the philosophy of his teacher in many ways.

If we want to understand the impact of Aristotle upon later thought, we must remember some curious facts connected with the transmission of his writings.[1] When Aristotle died in 322 B.C., he left a very extensive body of writings which consisted of two completely different groups. On the one hand, there was a large group of dialogues and other popular treatises which had been published during his lifetime, and which continued to be widely read through many centuries until they were finally lost towards the end of antiquity. These popular writings of Aristotle were praised for their literary elegance, and apparently the most famous among them were composed in Aristotle's earlier years and were comparatively close to Plato in their philosophical opinions. The second group of Aristotle's writings, which is the one that has come down to us, represents a collection of the lecture courses which he delivered in his school in Athens. These courses served no literary purpose, but in turn they are highly technical in character, very detailed in their reasoning and in the information supplied, and fairly systematic in their over-all arrangement, forming a vast encyclopaedia of philosophical and scientific knowledge. The systematic writings of Aristotle were not published by him or his immediate successors, but remained for several centuries in the library of his school where they were accessible to its professors, but not to the general public or to the members of other schools of philosophy. Apparently the Aristotelian corpus as we know it was published only between the first century B.C. and the first century A.D., and even some time after that date it does not seem to have been widely read or studied. Until the second century A.D., outside the circle of scholars trained in the Aristotelian school, the systematic writings of Aristotle exercised little or no influence upon the development of ancient thought, and it would be anachronistic to assume such an influence as a major factor in the Platonic Academy, in Stoicism, Epicureanism, or Skepticism, in Philo or in the early Christian thinkers. At the same time, the works and thoughts of Aristotle were transmitted, studied, interpreted, and supplemented by a long series of Aristotelian philosophers in his school, among whom the earliest, Theophrastus, and the last, Alexander of Aphrodisias, are best known to us. Alexander, who lived around 200 A.D., was one of the most authoritative commentators of Aristotle, and also modified the Aristotelian doctrine in a more naturalistic and anti-Platonic direction, denying, for example, the immortality of the soul, a point on which Aristotle had been somewhat ambiguous.

The rise of the Neoplatonic school, which was founded in the third century A.D. and dominated Greek thought down to the end of antiquity in the sixth century, also marks an important phase in the history of Aristotelianism. During that period, Aristotelianism disappeared as a separate school tradition, yet the Neoplatonists themselves were committed to a synthesis of Plato and Aristotle. Consequently, the systematic writings of Aristotle were no less thoroughly studied than the dialogues of Plato; Aristotelian doctrine, especially in logic and natural philosophy, was extensively appropriated, and some of the best and most voluminous commentaries on Aristotle, such as those of Simplicius, are due to members of this school. One Neoplatonic treatise,

Porphyry's introduction to the *Categories*, became almost an integral part of the Aristotelian corpus.

The fact that Aristotle was appropriated and in a sense preserved by the Neoplatonists left profound traces in the later history of Aristotelianism. In trying to follow this history through the Middle Ages, we must distinguish, as for all philosophical and scientific writings of Greek antiquity, three main traditions: the Byzantine, the Arabic, and the Latin.[2] The place of Aristotle in the Byzantine tradition has not yet been, to my knowledge, sufficiently investigated.[3] Yet it is apparent that the writings of the Aristotelian corpus were preserved and transmitted in their original Greek text by Byzantine scholars and copyists, and a number of extant Byzantine commentaries on Aristotle show that the study of his works and thought was by no means neglected. As far as I can make out, the study of Aristotle among the Byzantines was not separated from, or opposed to, the study of Plato and of the ancient Greek poets, or especially connected with theology, except for some very late authors who had been subjected to Western, Latin influences. If I am not mistaken, it was this Byzantine Aristotle, allied with Neoplatonism and literature and an integral part of the classical heritage, whom some of the Greek scholars of the fifteenth century carried along into their Italian exile and who exercised some influence upon the Aristotelian studies of the later Renaissance.

Very different, and for its impact upon the Western Middle Ages, more important, was the history of Aristotle among the Arabs.[4] When the Arabs began to translate the works of Greek literature that interested them, they largely omitted the Greek poets, orators, and historians, and centered their efforts on the most authoritative writers in such fields as mathematics and astronomy, medicine, astrology and alchemy, and philosophy. The translated Greek works provided the nucleus of subject matter in these disciplines, to which the Arabs subsequently added their own contributions. As far as philosophy is concerned, the Arabs acquired an almost complete corpus of Aristotle's systematic writings, along with some Neoplatonic and other commentaries on them, and with a certain number of Neoplatonic treatises. Thus the Arabs inherited Aristotle from the Neoplatonic tradition of late antiquity, and consequently, their understanding of Aristotle was affected by Neoplatonic interpretations and accretions which they were never able to eliminate completely. On the other hand, Aristotle attained among the Arabs an authority and doctrinal preponderance that he had never possessed in Greek antiquity to the very end. Apparently the Arabs did not acquire the complete writings of Plato and of the major Neoplatonists, and thus the sheer bulk of Aristotle's writings, along with their commentaries and with the apocrypha, outweighed all other Greek philosophical literature available to them. Moreover, these writings imposed themselves by the solidity of their content, and by the systematic and encyclopaedic character of the corpus, which lent itself to painstaking study and which comprised, besides such disciplines as logic, rhetoric, poetics, ethics, and metaphysics, also a number of others which have since been detached from philosophy as separate sciences, such as economics and psychology, physics and natural history. The Aristotelian corpus, supplemented by medicine and mathematics, seemed to represent a complete encyclopaedia of learning whose various writings coincided with the branches of knowledge as such. The authority of Aristotle was probably further enhanced by that of Galen, who was strongly influenced by Aristotelian philosophy and exercised a similar influence upon Arabic medicine, especially since some of the most important Arabic thinkers combined philosophy and medicine in their work. Thus the major Arabic philosophers, such as Avicenna and Averroes, were commentators and followers of Aristotle, and Averroes even tended to reduce the Neoplatonic additions and to attain a purer understanding of Aristotle. As is well known, the Aristotelianism of the Arabs, and especially that of Averroes, exercised a powerful influence upon the Jewish thought of the later Middle Ages, where Maimonides was the leading representative of Aristotelianism, and strongly affected the philosophy of the Christian West even after its tradition had come to a sudden end in the Islamic world itself, as a result of new religious and political developments.

If we want to understand the history of thought and learning in the Western Latin Middle Ages, we must first of all realize that it had its foundation in Roman, and not in Greek antiquity. The Romans produced, under the impact of Greek models, a distinguished literature in poetry and in prose; they appropriated the grammatical and rhetorical learning of the Greeks, and they made a lasting original contribution in the field of jurisprudence, but they did not develop a significant philosophical tradition. Rome and the other Western centers had flourishing schools of rhetoric, but no schools of philosophy comparable to those of Athens and Alexandria. The efforts to develop a technical vocabulary for philosophical discourse in the Latin language remained in the beginning stages until the end of antiquity. Few outstanding works of Greek philosophers were translated into Latin, and the philosophical literature produced by the Romans was mostly of a popularizing nature. Among the Greek sources of this literature Aristotle occupies a very minor place, compared with the Platonists, Stoics, Skeptics or Epicureans. He appears to be unknown to, or to have no importance for, Lucretius, Seneca, or St. Augustine; and even Cicero is chiefly acquainted with the published works of Aristotle that are now lost, and barely mentions the systematic writings which dominated the later tradition. The one significant exception is represented by one of the latest writers of Roman antiquity, Boethius, who translated at least two *c. 550 AD* of Aristotle's logical works, the *Categories* and the treatise *On Interpretation*, along with Porphyry's introduction.

During the early Middle Ages, the Latin West was largely cut off from the richer Greek tradition and reduced to the indigenous resources of Roman literature, which was weak in philosophy, as we have noticed. The body of secular learning provided in the monastic and cathedral schools of the period was limited to the elementary encyclopaedia of the seven liberal arts, that is, grammar, rhetoric, dialectic, arithmetic, geometry, astronomy, and music. In this scheme, which prevailed to the eleventh century, grammar was the leading subject, which included at times the study of the Latin poets. Philosophy was represented only by dialectic, that is, elementary logic, and this subject was largely based on the Aristotelian treatises translated by Boethius. Philosophy in the broad sense of the word as known to the ancient Greeks was almost forgotten, and the only author who made a genuine contribution to philosophical thought in that period, Scotus Eriugena, was an isolated figure distinguished for his acquaintance with Greek Neoplatonism.

This situation was completely changed through the remarkable rise of philosophical, theological, and scientific studies that began during the second half of the eleventh century and culminated in the thirteenth. During that period, the body of learning expanded steadily until it surpassed the traditional limits of the seven arts. A large amount of writings on philosophy, on the sciences and the pseudo sciences was translated from Arabic and from Greek that introduced precious material previously unavailable in Latin and tended to stimulate and transform Western thought.[5] Among the philosophical authors thus translated, Proclus and other Neoplatonic authors were well represented, but the most extensive and most important body of literature consisted of the nearly complete corpus of Aristotle, accompanied by a few Greek commentaries, and by a much larger body of Arabic commentaries, especially by Avicenna and Averroes. The writings of Aristotle and of his Greek commentators as well as of Proclus were in part translated from the original text, to be sure, but the selection of subjects and of authors clearly reflects the Arabic rather than the ancient Greek tradition of philosophy. At the same time, new institutions of higher learning developed, the universities, which differed considerably from the earlier schools in their curriculum, textbooks, and methods of instruction.[6] The instruction centered around the *lectura,* the continuous reading and exposition of a standard text, and the *disputatio,* the public discussion of a proposed thesis with the help of formalized arguments. These forms of instruction produced the two main types of medieval scholarly literature, the commentary and the question. The subject matter of university instruction was fixed during the thirteenth century at Paris and the other Northern universities in the system of four faculties, theology, law, medicine, and arts or philosophy. Whereas the teaching of theology was based on the Bible and on Peter Lombard's *Sentences,* and that of law on the Corpus Juris of Justinian and on Gratian's *Decretum,* the instruction in medicine and in philosophy came to be based on some of the new translations from the Greek and Arabic. The philosophical disciplines thus became for the first time in the Latin world subjects of separate instruction, and the texts adopted for this instruction, after some resistance, were the writings of Aristotle along with those of Averroes and of other commentators. The chief subjects were logic and natural philosophy, whereas ethics and metaphysics attained the status of elective courses only. Thus the writings of Aristotle had become by the middle of the thirteenth century the basis of philosophical instruction at the universities. They owed this position not merely to Arabic precedent, but also to the solidity of their content and to their systematic and encyclopaedic character. Aristotle was not studied as a "great book," but as a textbook that was the starting point for commentaries and questions and supplied a frame of reference for all trained philosophical thinkers even when they ventured to reinterpret him, or to depart from his doctrine, according to their own opinions. (The Aristotelianism of the later Middle Ages was characterized not so much by a common system of ideas as by a common source material, a common terminology, a common set of definitions and problems, and a common method of discussing these problems.) There was offered a variety of interpretations for many passages in Aristotle, and of solutions for the most debated problems, some of which grew out of medieval philosophical preoccupations rather than from Aristotle's own writings. The understanding of this vast and complex philosophical literature has made much progress in recent years, yet it is still hampered by the failure to distinguish clearly between philosophy and theology, which were separate disciplines, by an excessive faith in such general labels as Thomism, Scotism, Occamism, and Averroism, and by a tendency to focus attention too exclusively on St. Thomas Aquinas and his school. The Aristotelian philosophers of the thirteenth and fourteenth centuries were engaged in the discussion of numerous detailed problems, especially in logic and physics, and offered a great variety of solutions for each of them. Whereas it might be possible to group them roughly according to the stand taken on a particular issue, they may show a very different alignment with reference to some other issue.[7] Thomas Aquinas went farthest among his contemporaries in his attempt to reconcile Aristotelian philosophy and Christian theology, and his writings are distinguished by their clarity and coherence. Yet in his own time, he enjoyed no monopoly of authority or of orthodoxy; his teachings were in competition with many others, and sometimes even condemned, and much of his work belongs, by medieval standards, to theology rather than to philosophy.

His authority was soon established within his own Dominican order, but outside that order, the doctrines of Duns Scotus and of William of Ockham were much more influential, and the important developments in logic and physics which took place during the fourteenth century at Oxford and Paris were largely due to the Occamist school. Most ambiguous and controversial of all is the term Averroism which has been applied by historians to one particular trend of medieval Aristotelianism.[8] If we understand by Averroism the use of Averroes' commentary on Aristotle, every medieval Aristotelian including Aquinas was an Averroist. If we limit the term to all those thinkers who made a neat distinction between reason and faith, Aristotelian philosophy and Christian theology, practically all teachers of philosophy, as distinct from the theologians, took that position, from the later thirteenth century through the fourteenth and later. Finally, if we mean by Averroism the adherence to one distinctive doctrine of Averroes, namely the unity of the intellect in all men, we are singling out a much smaller group of thinkers who still differ among each other on the numerous other questions which occupied and divided the Aristotelian philosophers of the period. Hence it will be best to use these labels with great caution, and to emphasize the fact that the Aristotelian tradition of the later Middle Ages comprised a great variety of thinkers and of ideas held together by the common reference to the corpus of Aristotle's writings, which constituted the basic material of reading and discussion in the philosophical disciplines.

I seem to have given an undue share of my allotted time today to a discussion of medieval rather than Renaissance developments. Yet it has been my intention to show how Aristotle had become by the early fourteenth century "the master of those who know," in order to emphasize the additional fact, which is less widely known, that this Aristotelian tradition, though exposed to attacks and subject to transformations, continued strongly and vigorously to the end of the sixteenth century and even later. The failure to appreciate this fact is due to various reasons. Historians, like journalists, are apt to concentrate on news and to forget that there is a complex and broad situation which remained unaffected by the events of the moment. They also have for some time been more interested in the origins rather than in the continuations of intellectual and other developments. More specifically, many historians of thought have been sympathetic to the opponents of Aristotelianism in the Renaissance, whereas most of the defenders of medieval philosophy have limited their efforts to its earlier phases before the end of the thirteenth century, and have sacrificed the late scholastics to the critique of their contemporary and modern adversaries. Yet we have learned through recent studies that the chief progress made during the later fourteenth century in the fields of logic and natural philosophy was due to the Aristotelian, and more specifically, to the Occamist school at Paris and Oxford. During the fifteenth and sixteenth centuries, university instruction in the philosophical disciplines continued everywhere to be based on the works of Aristotle; consequently, most professional teachers of philosophy followed the Aristotelian tradition, used its terminology and method, discussed its problems, and composed commentaries and questions on Aristotle. Only a few individual thinkers and schools have been studied so far, and the large extent of this tradition, and of its proportional share in the philosophical literature of the Renaissance period, is not generally realized. This Aristotelian orientation of the university philosophers can be traced at Paris,[9] Louvain, and other centers far into the sixteenth century, although it has not been studied very much. It disappears from sight at Oxford and Cambridge after the end of the fourteenth century, but there is reason to believe that this is due to lack of scholarly attention rather than lack of facts or source materials.[9a] It flourished, in close alliance with Catholic theology, well into the seventeenth century at Salamanca, Alcalà, and Coimbra, and the influence of this Spanish neoscholasticism extended, through its most famous representative, Franciscus Suarez, well beyond the borders of the Iberian peninsula or of Catholicism.[10]   Also at the German universities, Aristotelianism was strong and productive through the fifteenth century, and continued to flourish long after the Protestant Reformation, for in spite of Luther's dislike for scholasticism, and thanks to the influence of <u>Melanchthon,</u> Aristotle remained the chief source of academic instruction in the philosophical disciplines.[11]   Thus it is not surprising if even later philosophers who turned far away from scholasticism, such as Bacon, Descartes, Spinoza, or Leibniz, still show in their terminology, in their arguments, and in some of their doctrines the traces of that tradition which was still alive in the schools and universities of their time, although we should realize that these thinkers absorbed at the same time also different influences which we might roughly describe as humanistic, Platonist, Stoic, or skeptical.[12]

We have not yet spoken about the place of Aristotelianism in Italy, a country which differed from the rest of Europe in many respects even during the Middle Ages and which occupied such an important position during the Renaissance period.   The customary views on the Italian Renaissance might easily lead us to believe that Aristotelian scholasticism flourished in medieval Italy as in the North, but was abandoned in Italy sooner than elsewhere under the impact of Renaissance humanism.   The actual facts suggest almost exactly the opposite.   Up to the last decades of the thirteenth century, instruction at the Italian universities was almost entirely limited to formal rhetoric, law, and medicine.   Scholastic theology was largely confined to the schools of the mendicant orders; and those famous scholastic theologians and philosophers who happened to be Italian, such as Lanfranc,

*But not "art" = philosophy

Anselm and Peter Lombard, St. Bonaventura and St. Thomas Aquinas, did most of their studying and teaching at Paris and other Northern centers. After some earlier appearance at Salerno and Naples, Aristotelian philosophy became for the first time firmly established at Bologna and other Italian universities towards the very end of the thirteenth century,[13] that is, at the same time that the first signs of a study of the Latin classics began to announce the coming rise of Italian humanism. Simultaneously with humanism, Italian Aristotelianism developed steadily through the fourteenth century under the influence of Paris and Oxford, became more independent and more productive through the fifteenth century,[14] and attained its greatest development during the sixteenth and early seventeenth centuries, in such comparatively well known thinkers as Pomponazzi, Zabarella, and Cremonini. In other words, as far as Italy is concerned, Aristotelian scholasticism, just like classical humanism, is fundamentally a phenomenon of the Renaissance period whose ultimate roots can be traced in a continuous development to the very latest phase of the Middle Ages. The greatest difference between this Italian Aristotelianism and its Northern counterpart, aside from the times of their respective rise and decline, is related to the organization of the universities and their faculties or schools. In Paris and the other Northern centers, philosophy was taught in the faculty of arts, which also included what was left of the seven liberal arts, and which served as preparation for the three higher faculties of law, medicine, and theology, and especially for the latter. (At Bologna and the other Italian centers, there were only two faculties, that of law and that of the arts.) There never was a separate faculty of theology. Within the faculty of arts, medicine was the most important subject of instruction, logic and natural philosophy were considered as preparatory for medicine and occupied the second place, whereas grammar, rhetoric, and moral philosophy, mathematics and astronomy, theology and metaphysics came last. As in the North, logic and natural philosophy were considered the most important philosophical disciplines and taught on the basis of Aristotle and his commentators, but this instruction was and always remained linked with medicine and unrelated to theology.

Under the misleading name of "Paduan Averroism," some phases of this Italian Aristotelianism have been studied during the last hundred years or so, but much of the literature produced by it remains unpublished or unread. It consists in commentaries and questions on the works of Aristotle, and in independent treatises on related problems. The labels used for it such as Thomism, Scotism and Occamism, Averroism and Alexandrism are, as usual, inadequate. Their work consists, like that of their Northern predecessors and contemporaries, in a detailed discussion of many minute questions where each particular issue was likely to produce a variety of solutions and a different alignment of individual thinkers. Again they agree in their method and terminology, and in their constant reference to Aristotle and his commentators, but there are few philosophical doctrines common to all of them. The separation between philosophy and theology, reason or Aristotle and faith or religious authority, was consistently maintained, without leading to a direct conflict or opposition. Besides rational argument, sense perception or experience was emphasized as the major or only source of natural knowledge, and this might justify us in speaking of a kind of empiricism. In the sixteenth century, Averroes' doctrine of the unity of the intellect for all men continued to be discussed, although it was accepted only by some of the Aristotelian philosophers. At the same time, the related problem of immortality became the center of discussion through a famous and controversial treatise of Pomponazzi, who rejected the unity of the intellect but maintained that the immortality of the soul cannot be demonstrated on rational or Aristotelian principles. (Later Aristotelians such as Zabarella participated in the discussion on the nature of the cognitive method, and formulated the doctrine that natural knowledge proceeds through analysis from the observed phenomena to their inferred causes, and returns through synthesis from the latter to the former, a doctrine that was at least partly rooted in the Aristotelian tradition and influenced in turn so anti-Aristotelian a scientist as Galileo.[15]) Among the Aristotelian philosophers of the Italian Renaissance, the strongest influences were apparently those of Occamism and of the so-called Averroism, which were gradually modified by various contemporary developments. At the same time, Thomism and Scotism continued to flourish among the theologians. Scotism seems to have been the more active and more widely diffused current, but the Italian Renaissance produced such authoritative Thomists as Caietanus, and the Dominican teaching affected many other theologians, and also such non-Thomist philosophers as Ficino and Pomponazzi. If we add to this the authority attached to Thomas by the Jesuits and by the Council of Trent, and the increasing use of his *Summa*, instead of Peter Lombard's *Sentences*, as a textbook of theology,[16] we may very well say that the sixteenth century marks a notable advance over the thirteenth and fourteenth centuries in the relaive role and importance of Thomism, and a conspicuous step towards that adoption of Thomism as the official philosophy of the Catholic Church which was finally codified in 1879.

After this all-too-brief discussion of Renaissance Aristotelianism in its close relations to the later Middle Ages, I should like to mention those changes and modifications which it underwent under the impact of the new attitudes of the period, and especially of classical humanism. The keynote of this change was sounded by Petrarch when he suggested that Aristotle was better than his translators and commentators, and the general tendency was to take Aristotle out of his isolation as a textbook authority into the company of the other ancient philosophers and writers.[17] Western scholars learned from their Byzantine teachers to study the works of Aristotle in the Greek original. Humanist professors began to lecture on Aristotle as one of the classical Greek authors, and Aristotelian philosophers who had enjoyed a humanist education were led to refer to the original text of their chief authority. Although practically the whole corpus of Aristotle's works had been translated into Latin during the later Middle Ages, the Renaissance humanists used their increased knowledge of the Greek language and literature to supply new Latin versions of Aristotle which competed with their medieval predecessors and gradually penetrated into the university curriculum. The merits of these humanist translations in relation to the medieval ones have been debated ever since their own time, and obviously vary according to the abilities of the individual translators. They show a better knowledge of syntax, idioms, and textual variants, and also a greater freedom in word order, style, and terminology. The changes in terminology were a serious matter in an author who served as a standard text in philosophy, and the net result was to present an Aristotle who was different from that of the medieval tradition. Moreover, there were a few additions made to the Aristotelian corpus, and some of the writings previously available acquired a novel importance or a novel place in the system of learning. The *Eudemian Ethics* was translated for the first time, and so were the *Mechanics* and some other writings of the early Aristotelian school. The *Theology* of Aristotle, an apocryphal work of Arabic origin and Neoplatonic tendency, was used to emphasize the agreement between Plato and Aristotle, and the fragments of Aristotle's lost early writings were collected for the same purpose.[18] The humanists who considered moral philosophy as a part of their domain and often held the chair of

ethics continued to use the *Nicomachean Ethics* and *Politics*
as their main texts, and thus were led to give to Aristotle's
doctrine an important share in their eclectic views on moral,
educational, and political questions. Aristotle's *Rhetoric,*
which in the Middle Ages had been neglected by the professional rhetoricians and treated by the scholastic philosophers as an appendix to the *Ethics* and *Politics,*[19] became
during the sixteenth century an important text for the humanist rhetoricians. The *Poetics,* not completely unknown
to the Latin Middle Ages,[20] as scholars had long believed,
but still comparatively neglected, attained through the humanists a wide circulation and became in the sixteenth century the standard text which gave rise to a large body of
critical discussion and literature;[21] and it is curious to note
that the authority of Aristotle's *Poetics* attained its climax
in the same seventeenth century which witnessed the overthrow of his *Physics.* Finally, if we pass from the humanist scholars to the professional philosophers and scientists,
it appears that the most advanced work of Aristotle's logic,
the *Posterior Analytics,* received greater attention in the
sixteenth century than before, and that at the same time an
increased study of Aristotle's biological writings accompanied the contemporary progress in botany, zoology, and
natural history.[22]

With reference to those works of Aristotle which were
and remained the center of instruction in logic and natural
philosophy, the most important changes derived from the
fact that the works of the ancient Greek commentators became completely available in Latin between the late fifteenth and the end of the sixteenth centuries and were more
and more used to balance the interpretations of the medieval
Arabic and Latin commentators. The Middle Ages had
known their works only in a very limited selection or through
quotations in Averroes. Ermolao Barbaro's complete
translation of Themistius and Girolamo Donato's version,

of Alexander's *De anima* were among the most important ones in a long line of others. ((When modern historians speak of Alexandrism as a current within Renaissance Aristotelianism that was opposed to Averroism, they are justified in part by the fact that the Greek commentators, that is, Alexander and also Themistius, Simplicius, and many others, were increasingly drawn upon for the exposition of Aristotle.)) In a more particular sense, Alexander's specific notion that the human soul was mortal received more attention from the Aristotelian philosophers. Thus the change and increase in Aristotelian source material led in many instances to a doctrinal change in the interpretation of the philosopher or in the philosophical position defended in the name of reason, nature, and Aristotle, and these doctrinal changes were further enhanced under the impact of both classical and contemporary ideas of different, non-Aristotelian origin. ((Thus Pomponazzi, who is rightly considered an outstanding representative of the Aristotelian school, emphasizes such non-Aristotelian doctrines as the central position of man in the universe and the importance of the practical rather than the speculative intellect for human happiness, which are both of humanistic origin; defends the Stoic doctrine of fate against Alexander of Aphrodisias; and follows Plato and the Stoics in stressing that moral virtue is its own reward, vice its own greatest punishment.[23])) Such amalgamations of diverse doctrines are bound to occur in any genuine philosophical tradition dedicated to the pursuit of truth rather than of orthodoxy, and they become harmful only when they are used to distort the historical facts or to bolster the dogmatic claims of a particular tradition. The gradual nature of the change which affected Renaissance Aristotelianism and which I have been trying to describe is apparent when we compare the works of two outstanding Aristotelian philosophers of the early and of the late sixteenth century. Jacopo Zabarella, who represents the later phase, had acquired a full command of the Greek Aristotle and of his ancient commentators, and thus he has been praised by modern scholars not only as a good philosopher, but also as one of the best and most lucid Aristotelian commentators of all ages. Pietro Pomponazzi, who died in 1525, knew no Greek and was still deeply imbued with the traditions of medieval Aristotelianism, but he eagerly seized upon the new source material made available by his humanist contemporaries, and derived from Alexander the idea that the immortality of the human soul could not be demonstrated on rational or Aristotelian principles. Thus the classical scholarship of the humanists, applied to Aristotle and to his Greek commentators, had an indirect but powerful effect upon the continuing tradition of philosophical Aristotelianism through the sixteenth century and afterwards.

Our picture of the Renaissance attitude towards Aristotle would be incomplete if we failed to discuss the strong currents of anti-Aristotelianism which have been often exaggerated or misunderstood but which do occupy an important place in Renaissance thought. The rebellion against the authority of Aristotle or at least against his medieval interpreters is indeed a recurrent feature in the writings of many Renaissance thinkers from Petrarch to Bruno and Galileo. When we examine this polemic in each case for its reasons, content, and results, instead of taking its charges and claims at their face value, we are led to the conclusion that the anti-Aristotelianism of the Renaissance laid the ground for certain later developments, to be sure, but that it was in its own time neither unified nor effective. When we listen to Petrarch's attacks against Aristotle and his medieval followers, we are apt to forget that the Aristotelianism which he attacked had been established at the universities for hardly a hundred years, and in Italy even more recently. Thus a younger generation tends to believe that it is overthrowing a tradition of many centuries when in fact this tradition had been barely established by its fathers or grandfathers. The humanist attacks against scholasticism from which Aristotle himself was often exempted are known from several documents of the fifteenth century, from Leonardo Bruni to Ermolao Barbaro.[24] (This polemic turned out to be ineffective inasmuch as the humanists criticized the bad style of their opponents, their ignorance of classical sources, and their preoccupation with supposedly unimportant questions, but failed to make positive contributions to the philosophical and scientific disciplines with which the scholastics were concerned.) If we keep in mind the cultural and professional divisions of the period, and the flourishing state of Aristotelian philosophy in Renaissance Italy, we are inclined to view this polemic in its proper perspective, that is, as an understandable expression of departmental rivalry, and as a phase in the everlasting battle of the arts of which many other examples may be cited from ancient, medieval, or modern times.[25] Only in some instances did Renaissance humanists succeed in attacking their scholastic opponents on their own ground. There was a persistent tendency which began with Valla and culminated in Ramus and Nizolius to reform Aristotelian logic with the help of rhetoric, and during the latter part of the sixteenth century as well as much of the seventeenth, Ramism was a serious rival of Aristotelian logic in the schools of Germany, Great Britain, and America.[26] On the other hand, the Spanish humanist Vives made the ambitious attempt to substitute a classical and humanist encyclopaedia of learning for the medieval one and exercised a deep and wide influence on Western education.[27]

(Renaissance Platonism, which many historians have been inclined to oppose to medieval Aristotelianism, was not as persistently anti-Aristotelian as we might expect.) Its most influential representatives were either impressed by the

Neoplatonic synthesis of Plato and Aristotle, or even directly affected by medieval Aristotelianism. (Thus Marsilio Ficino would follow both Plato and Aristotle, though according the higher place to Plato, a view which is reflected in Raphael's School of Athens, and Pico della Mirandola expressly defended the medieval Aristotelians against the humanist attacks of Ermolao Barbaro.[28])

It was only during the sixteenth century that Aristotelianism began to be attacked in its central territory, that is, in natural philosophy. A series of brilliant thinkers, not unaffected by Aristotelianism or other traditions, but original in their basic intention, people like Paracelsus, Telesio, Patrizi, Bruno, and others,[29] began to propose rival systems of cosmology and of natural philosophy which made an impression upon their contemporaries and have been of lasting interest to historians of Renaissance thought. They failed to overthrow the Aristotelian tradition in natural philosophy, not because they were persecuted, or because their opponents preferred vested interests and habits of thought to the truth, but because their impressive doctrines were not based on a firm and acceptable method. Aristotelian natural philosophy, rich in subject matter and solid in concepts, could not possibly be displaced from the university curriculum as long as there was no comparable body of teachable doctrine that could have taken its place. This was not supplied by the humanists, the Platonists, or the natural philosophers of the later Renaissance, who could dent but not break the Aristotelian tradition. The decisive attack upon the natural philosophy of the Aristotelians came from Galileo and the other physicists of the seventeenth century.

This momentous event in the history of modern thought has often been represented rather crudely as a victory of "Science" and the "Scientific Method" over superstition or a mistaken tradition. There is no such thing as Science or the Scientific Method, but there is a complex body of various sciences and other forms of knowledge whose unity remains an ideal program, and there are various methods of attaining valid knowledge and of judging its validity. In the period preceding Galileo with which we are concerned, the various sciences differed in their traditions and mutual relations. Mathematics and astronomy were largely separate from philosophy and the Aristotelian tradition, and made notable advances during the sixteenth century without affecting that tradition in a serious way.[30] Medicine was another science distinct from philosophy, but more closely linked to it since medicine and philosophy were considered as parts of the same study and career, and since such medical authorities as Galen and Avicenna were Aristotelians. Nevertheless, notable progress was made in such medical disciplines as anatomy and surgery, that were based on observation and comparatively removed from the philosophical and medical theories of the time. On the other hand, natural philosophy as then understood and taught from the works of Aristotle, comprised such sciences as physics and biology. Even the development of these two sciences took a different course with reference to Aristotelianism. In biology, great progress was made during the sixteenth century and even afterwards within the framework of the Aristotelian tradition. In physics, on the other hand, the very conception of Aristotelian physics had to be overthrown in order to make room for modern physics. The Aristotelian physics of the later Middle Ages and of the Renaissance was not as wrong or absurd as older scholars had assumed, nor was Galileo as unaffected by it as he himself or some of his modern admirers believed.[31] Yet for the Aristotelians, physics was a matter of qualities, not of quantities, and its objects on earth were essentially different from the stars in heaven. Consequently, Aristotelian physics was closely linked with formal logic, but separated from mathematics and even to some extent from astronomy.

Contrast with B.

Galileo, the professional mathematician and astronomer who claimed to be a natural philosopher, postulated a new physics based on experiments and calculations, a physics of quantities that had for its foundation not formal logic, but mathematics, and that was to be closely related to astronomy.[32] Once this new physics had been firmly established in its methods and had begun to yield more and more specific results, it was bound to undermine the prestige of traditional Aristotelian physics and eventually to drive it from its place in the curriculum. This happened during the seventeenth and early eighteenth centuries, and it could not possibly have happened in the sixteenth. Our impatient enthusiasm for the achievements of a later period should not prompt us to read them back into an earlier epoch, or to blame the latter for not having anticipated them. To be sure, individual thinkers are always capable of startling insights, but a large group of people is likely to change its modes of thought rather slowly unless it is suddenly shaken by fashion, by violent experiences, or by political compulsion.

Thus we may conclude that the authority of Aristotle was challenged during the Renaissance in different ways and for different reasons, but that it remained quite strong, especially in the field of natural philosophy. This was due not so much to professional inertia as to the wealth and solidity of subject matter contained in the Aristotelian writings, to which its critics for some time could not oppose anything comparable. The concepts and methods that were bound to overthrow Aristotelian physics were just being discussed and prepared during the sixteenth century, but did not bear visible and lasting fruits before the seventeenth. The anti-Aristotelian revolution which marks the beginning of the modern period in the physical sciences and in philosophy had some of its roots and forerunners in the Renaissance period, but did not actually occur until later.

The Renaissance is still in many respects an Aristotelian age which in part continued the trends of medieval Aristotelianism, and in part gave it a new direction under the influence of classical humanism and other different ideas.

3. RENAISSANCE PLATONISM

PLATO'S influence on Western thought has been so broad and profound, and in spite of occasional voices of dissent, so continuous, that a great contemporary thinker has been able to state that the history of Western philosophy may be characterized as a series of footnotes to Plato.[1] Yet if we examine the actual ideas of those thinkers who have professed their indebtedness to the Athenian philosopher or who have been called Platonists by themselves or by others, we do not only find, as might be expected, a series of different interpretations and reinterpretations of Plato's teachings and writings. We are also confronted with the puzzling fact that different Platonists have selected, emphasized, and developed different doctrines or passages from Plato's works. Hardly a single notion which we associate with Plato has been held by all Platonists, neither the transcendent existence of universal forms nor the direct knowledge of these intelligible entities, neither spiritual love nor the immortality of the soul, let alone his outline of the perfect state. Thus it is possible for two thinkers who have been conventionally and perhaps legitimately classified as Platonists to have very different philosophies, or even to have not a single specific doctrine in common. The term Platonism does not lend itself very well as a middle term to the arithmetic or syllogistics of sources and influences, unless the specific texts and notions involved in each case are spelled out in all their detail. Moreover, ever since classical antiquity, Platonist philosophers have tried not so much to repeat or restate Plato's doctrines in their original form, as to combine them with notions of diverse origin, and these accretions, like the tributaries of a broadening river, became integral parts of the continuing tradition. They are as necessary for a proper understanding of the history of Platonism, as they might be misleading if used uncritically for an interpretation of Plato himself. It is only during the last 150 years or so that modern scholarship has attempted to cleanse the genuine thought of Plato from the mire of the Platonic tradition. This effort has yielded in part very solid results, yet today we are beginning to feel that there has been a tendency to exaggerate the differences between Plato and later Platonism, and to overlook certain genuine features in Plato's thought that may be alien to modern science and philosophy, but served as a starting point for his earlier interpreters.[2] Thus an archaeologist who tries to remove the crust of later centuries from a Greek statue must be careful not to damage its incomparably subtle surface.

This complex and even elusive nature of the Platonic tradition is partly due to the character of Plato's thought and writings. Among all major Greek philosophers until Plotinus, Plato had the unique fortune of having his works, as far as we can tell, completely preserved. These works are literary compositions written and published in different periods of a long and eventful life. They are in the form of dialogues which sometimes end without apparent conclusion and in which different views are proposed and discussed by different persons. Since Plato rarely speaks in his own name, it seems difficult to identify his own definite opinions, or to separate them from those of Socrates, Parmenides, and his other characters. Moreover, some of the most coherent passages are presented in the ambiguous form of myths, similes, or digressions. Finally, the different dialogues, though not completely unrelated in their subject matter, fail to suggest any order or connection that might lead to a philosophical system. Modern scholarship has tried to overcome these difficulties through the historical method, to establish a chronological sequence for the authentic dialogues, and to supplement their content with the statements of Aristotle and others about Plato's oral teaching. This historical approach was foreign to the Platonist scholars of classical antiquity. They merely collected all works attributed to Plato in a single edition, thus giving them the appearance of a systematic order which to us seems artificial. In this manner, a number of apocryphal pieces found their way into the Platonic corpus and continued to influence the subsequent tradition, although the authenticity of certain Platonic works was already questioned in antiquity.

Plato's influence upon later Greek thought was dependent not only on his dialogues which were generally available to the reading public, but also on the school which he founded and which continued as an institution for many centuries until 529 A.D. Since Plato left no systematic writings to his school, and since even his oral teaching was apparently not of a dogmatic character, the philosophical tradition in his Academy was subject to much greater changes and fluctuations than in the other philosophical schools of antiquity. Plato's immediate successors in the Academy modified his doctrine as we know it hardly less than did another pupil, Aristotle,[3] and during the third century B.C. the Academy turned towards a more or less radical skepticism to which it clung for more than two hundred years. In the meantime, Plato's dialogues were read and admired outside his school, and strongly affected the thought of such Stoic philosophers as Panaetius and Posidonius. Around the beginning of our era, a popular and somewhat eclectic kind of Platonism that borrowed various elements from Aristotle and especially from Stoicism had replaced Skepticism in the Athenian Academy, had established a kind of school in Alexandria and perhaps in other centers, and had begun to pervade the thought of a widening circle of philosophical and popular writers.[4] This movement, which is now commonly called Middle Platonism, made at least one important contribution to the history of Platonism, for it formulated the doctrine, ever since attributed to Plato but hardly found in his dialogues, that the (transcendent ideas or intelligible forms are concepts of a divine intelligence.) Middle Platonism had many elements in common with the Neopythagoreanism which flourished during the first centuries of our era and forged many Platonizing works under the name of Pythagoras and his early pupils, and with the Hermetics, a circle of pagan theologians who flourished in Alexandria and composed a corpus of writings that were attributed to the Egyptian divinity Hermes Trismegistus.[5] When Philo the Jew, and after him the Alexandrian Church Fathers Clement and Origen, made the first attempts to combine the teachings of Biblical religion with Greek philosophy, it was the Platonism popular at their time which supplied the most numerous and most important doctrinal elements. Thus the ground was well prepared both among pagans and Christians when philosophical Platonism was revived during the third century A.D. in Alexandria by Ammonius Saccas and by his great pupil, Plotinus.

This school, which called itself Platonic and which modern historians have named Neoplatonic to emphasize its differences from Plato, chose Plato's dialogues for its chief philosophical authority, but tried to fit Plato's scattered doctrines into a coherent system and to incorporate in it other ideas derived from the Stoics and especially from Aristotle. As a comprehensive synthesis of Greek thought, Neoplatonism thus dominated the latest phase of ancient philosophy and bequeathed its heritage to subsequent ages. Beneath the surface of the common school tradition, there are many significant differences of doctrine that have not yet been fully explored. To the genuine elements derived from Plato, Plotinus added a more explicit emphasis on a hierarchical universe that descends through several levels from the transcendent God or One to the corporeal world, and on an inner, spiritual experience that enables the self to reascend through the intelligible world to that supreme One; whereas the physical world is conceived, probably under the influence of Posidonius, as a web of hidden affinities originating in a world soul and other cosmic souls. In Proclus, one of the last heads of the Athenian school, Neoplatonism attains its most systematic and even schematic perfection. In his *Elements of Theology* and *Platonic Theology* all things and their mutual relations are neatly defined and deduced in their proper place and order; and the concepts of Aristotle's logic and metaphysics, divested of their specific and concrete reference, are used as elements of a highly abstract and comprehensive ontology.[6] As a commentator, Proclus applied this neat and scholastic system to some of Plato's dialogues, just as other members of the school applied it to Aristotle. And as the leading philosophy of the period, Neoplatonism supplied practically all later Greek Church Fathers and theologians with their philosophical terms and concepts, most of all that obscure father of most Christian mysticism who hides under the name of Dionysius the Areopagite, and whose writings owed a tremendous authority to the name of their supposed author, a direct disciple of St. Paul the Apostle.

The Platonic tradition during the Middle Ages, which has been the subject of much recent study, followed again three different lines of development.[7] In the Byzantine East, the original works of Plato and of the Neoplatonists were always available, and the study of Plato was surely often combined with that of the ancient Greek poets and of Aristotle.[8] The prevalence of Plato over Aristotle within a synthesis of both was justified by Neoplatonic precedent, and the tendency to harmonize Plato rather than Aristotle with Christian theology was amply sanctioned by the Greek patristic authors. In the eleventh century, Michael Psellus revived the interest in Platonic philosophy, and set an influential precedent by combining with it the *Chaldaic Oracles* attributed to Zoroaster, and·the *Corpus Hermeticum*. In the fourteenth and fifteenth centuries, Gemistus Pletho attempted another revival of Plato's philosophy based on Proclus and Psellus. He even aimed at a philosophical reform of the falling Greek Empire, and gave, after the model of Proclus, an allegorical explanation of the Greek divinities, which exposed him to the charge that he wanted to restore ancient paganism.[9] Certainly he was convinced that Plato and his ancient followers were the representatives of a very old pagan theology which has for its witnesses the writings attributed to Hermes Trismegistus and Zoroaster, Orpheus and Pythagoras, and which parallels both in age and content the revelation of the Hebrew and Christian Scriptures. Through his teaching and writings, through his pupils, and through the violent reaction of his theological and Aristotelian opponents, Pletho did a good deal to awaken Platonic scholarship and philosophy in the Byzantine Empire during its last decades; and thanks to Pletho's stay in Italy and to the activities of his pupil, Cardinal Bessarion, and of other Greek scholars devoted or opposed to him, this development had important repercussions in the West until and beyond the end of the fifteenth century.[10]

Among the Arabs, Plato's position was inferior to that of Aristotle and consequently less important than in antiquity or in the Byzantine Middle Ages.[11] Whereas the corpus of Aristotle was almost completely translated into Arabic, only a few works of Plato, such as the *Republic,* the *Laws,* and the *Timaeus,* were made available, supplemented by a number of other Platonist writings. On the other hand, the Arabs derived many Platonist conceptions from the Aristotelian commentators, and they possessed at least two Aristotelian apocrypha, the *Liber de causis* and the *Theologia Aristotelis,* whose doctrinal content was based entirely on Proclus and Plotinus. Arabic philosophers such as Alfarabi wrote a paraphrase of Plato's *Laws,* and even the faithful Aristotelian commentator, Averroes, composed a paraphrase of Plato's *Republic.* Under the influence of the Arabic tradition, medieval Jewish thought included a strong neoplatonic current. Avicebron (ibn Gabirol), whose *Fountain of Life* exercised a strong influence in its Latin version also belongs to this tradition, and the peculiar form of medieval Jewish mysticism known as the Cabala contains several ideas derived from Neoplatonic and other late ancient philosophies.[12] Moreover, among both the Arabs and their Jewish disciples, the occult sciences of astrology, alchemy, and magic were cultivated in close connection with the genuine philosophical and scientific disciplines. These pseudo sciences also derived their traditions from the later phases of Greek antiquity, and they were or became associated with Platonist and Hermetic philosophy, with which they actually shared such notions as the world soul and the belief in the numerous hidden powers or specific affinities and antipathies of all things natural.

Roman antiquity, though poor in specific philosophical achievements, as we have seen, gave a larger share to the Platonic tradition than it did to Aristotle. Cicero, who had been a student at the Athenian Academy, reflected in his philosophical writings not only the Skepticism which had dominated that school for several centuries, but also the first phases of that eclectic or Middle Platonism which was just beginning to replace it. Further Middle Platonic ideas appear in Apuleius, occasionally in Seneca, and in Chalcidius' commentary on the *Timaeus;* whereas Neoplatonism was the basis for the writings of Macrobius, and for Boethius' influential *Consolation of Philosophy.* Of Plato's own works, Latin readers possessed only the partial versions of the *Timaeus* due to Cicero and Chalcidius; the version of Plotinus attributed to Victorinus was probably not extensive, and certainly did not survive very long. The most important representative of Platonism in ancient Latin literature was St. Augustine, who acknowledged his debt to Plato and Plotinus more frankly than most of his modern theological admirers.[13] Typical Platonist doctrines, such as the eternal presence of the universal forms in the mind of God, the immediate comprehension of these ideas by human reason, and the incorporeal nature and the immortality of the human soul, are persistently asserted in his earlier philosophical as well as in his later theological writings, and they do not become less Platonist because they are combined with different Biblical or specifically Augustinian conceptions or because Augustine rejected other Platonic or Neoplatonic doctrines that seemed incompatible with the Christian dogma. Augustine's repeated assertion that Platonism is closer to Christian doctrine than any other pagan philosophy went a long way to justify later attempts to combine or reconcile them with each other.

During the early Middle Ages, when philosophical studies were not much cultivated in Western Europe, the most important text translated from the Greek was the corpus of writings attributed to Dionysius the Areopagite, who was also identified with the patron saint of St. Denis near Paris.[14] And the only author who had philosophical significance, Johannes Scotus Eriugena, was strongly imbued with Neoplatonic conceptions which were accessible to him in their original Greek sources. When philosophical studies began to flourish with the rise of scholasticism after the middle of the eleventh century, Augustinianism, which comprised many Platonist elements, became the prevailing current. This was quite natural, since the writings of Augustine represented the most solid body of philosophical and theological ideas then available in Latin. It was supplemented by Boethius' *Consolation,* by his logical works and his translations from Aristotle and Porphyry, and by Chalcidius' partial translation and commentary of Plato's *Timaeus.* There was thus a body of source material available for philosophical study before the new translations from the Arabic and Greek were added, and this material was for the most part Platonist in character, and included at least one work of Plato, the *Timaeus.* Hence it is significant that in one of the most important centers of early scholasticism, at the cathedral school of Chartres, the *Timaeus* was apparently used as a textbook in natural philosophy, as a number of glosses and commentaries coming from that school would seem to indicate.[15] And a strange and long neglected Platonist work, the so-called *Altividius,* seems to have been composed during the same century.[16] When the new translations brought about a vast increase in philosophical and scientific literature, Aristotle and his commentators gradually gained the upper hand, as we have seen, and hence during the thirteenth century Aristotelianism became the prevailing current of Western thought. Yet at the same time, Platonism also profited from the new translating activity. The versions from the Greek included two dialogues of Plato, the *Phaedo* and the *Meno,* the work of Nemesius of Emesa, and a number of treatises by Proclus, such as the *Elements of Theology* and the commentary on the *Parmenides,* which contains part of Plato's own text.[17] On the other hand, we find among the versions from the Arabic not only the Aristotelian commentators who contained much Neoplatonic material, but also the *Liber de Causis,* Avicebron's *Fons vitae,* and a vast amount of astrological and alchemical literature that transmitted, or pretended to transmit, many notions of Platonist or Hermetic origin. Hence we are not surprised to find Augustinian or Neoplatonic notions even in the thought of many Aristotelian philosophers of the thirteenth and early fourteenth centuries. On the other hand, the Augustinian tradition persisted as a secondary current during that period, and the speculative mysticism of Master Eckhart and his school drew much of its inspiration from the Areopagite, Proclus, and other Neoplatonic sources.

During the Renaissance, these medieval currents continued in many quarters. German speculative mysticism was succeeded in the Low Countries by the more practical *Devotio Moderna* which exercised a wide influence in Northern Europe.[18] The Augustinian trend in theology and metaphysics went on without interruption; the increasing religious literature for laymen contained strong Augustinian elements, and even some of the Platonizing works written in Chartres during the twelfth century still found attentive readers. Yet although several elements of medieval Platonism survived during the Renaissance, it would be wrong to overlook the novel or different aspects of Renaissance Platonism. They were partly due to the impact of Byzantine thought and learning, for the Eastern scholars who came to Italy for a temporary or permanent residence after the middle of the fourteenth century familiarized their Western pupils with Plato's writings and teachings, and with the controversy on the merits of Plato and Aristotle. While Chrysoloras was staying in Italy, he suggested the first Latin translation of Plato's *Republic*. Pletho's visit in Florence in 1438 left a deep impression, and the debate on Plato and Aristotle was continued in Italy by his pupils and opponents and by their Western followers. The most important document of the controversy is Bessarion's defense of Plato which drew on Western sources and which exercised some influence until the sixteenth century.[19] Other documents related to this debate have but recently attracted attention, or are still in need of further exploration.

Even more important was the impulse given by the Italian humanists of the period. Petrarch was not well ac-

quainted with Plato's works or philosophy, but he was the
first Western scholar who owned a Greek manuscript of
Plato sent to him by a Byzantine colleague,[20] and in his attack on the authority of Aristotle among the philosophers
of his time, he used at least Plato's name. This program
was then carried out by his humanist successors. They
studied Plato in the Greek original, and many of the dialogues were for the first time translated into Latin during the
first half of the fifteenth century, including such works as the
Republic, the *Laws,* the *Gorgias* and part of the *Phaedrus.*
Some of these translations, like those of Leonardo Bruni,
attained great popularity.[21]   Other Platonist authors of antiquity were also made available in new Latin versions, and
in the eclectic thought of the literary humanists Plato and
his ancient followers occupied their appropriate place.
Finally, at a time when a revival of everything ancient was
the order of the day, and when restatements of many ancient philosophies were being attempted as a philosophical
sequel to classical humanism, a revival of Platonism in one
form or another was bound to occur.

However, Renaissance Platonism, in spite of its close
links with classical humanism, cannot be understood as a
mere part or offshoot of the humanistic movement. It pos-
sesses independent significance as a philosophical, not merely as a scholarly or literary, movement; it is connected both
with the Augustinian and Aristotelian traditions of medieval philosophy; and thanks to the work of three major
thinkers of the late fifteenth century, it became a major
factor in the intellectual history of the sixteenth, and even
afterwards. The earliest and greatest of the three, Nico-
laus Cusanus, was indebted to German and Dutch mysticism as well as to Italian humanism.[22] In his philosophical
thought, which has many original features, notions derived
from Plato, Proclus, and the Areopagite play a major part.
He interprets the ideas in the divine mind as a single arche-

type which expresses itself in each particular thing in a different way, and he stresses the certainty and exemplary status of pure mathematical knowledge, to mention only a few facets of his complex thought that show his link with the Platonic tradition. The most central and most influential representative of Renaissance Platonism is Marsilius Ficinus, in whom the medieval philosophical and religious heritage and the teachings of Greek Platonism are brought together in a novel synthesis.[28] As a translator, he gave to the West the first complete version of Plato and of Plotinus in Latin, adding several other Neoplatonic writings; and in adopting Pletho's conception of a pagan theological tradition before Plato, he translated also the works attributed to Pythagoras and Hermes Trismegistus that were bound to share the popularity and influence of Renaissance Platonism. In his *Platonic Theology* he gave to his contemporaries an authoritative summary of Platonist philosophy, in which the immortality of the soul is emphasized, reasserting to some extent the Thomist position against the Averroists. His Platonic Academy with its courses and discussions provided for some decades an institutional center whose influence was spread all over Europe through his letters and other writings. Assigning to the human soul the central place in the hierarchy of the universe, he gave a metaphysical expression to a notion dear to his humanist predecessors; whereas his doctrine of spiritual love in Plato's sense, for which he coined the term Platonic love, became one of the most popular concepts of later Renaissance literature. His emphasis on the inner ascent of the soul towards God through contemplation links him with the mystics, whereas his doctrine of the unity of the world brought about by the soul influenced the natural philosophers of the sixteenth century.

Closely associated with the Florentine Academy, but in many ways different from Ficino, was his younger contemporary, Giovanni Pico della Mirandola.[24] In his thought, which did not reach full maturity, the attempt was made to achieve a synthesis between Platonism and Aristotelianism. His curiosity encompassed also Arabic and Hebrew language and thought, and as the first Western scholar who became acquainted with the Jewish Cabala, he made the influential attempt to reconcile the Cabala with Christian theology and to associate it with the Platonist tradition. His *Oration* on the dignity of man became the most famous expression of that humanist credo to which he gave a novel philosophical interpretation in terms of man's freedom to choose his own destiny.[25]

The place of Platonism in sixteenth-century thought is rather complex and difficult to describe.[26] Unlike humanism or Aristotelianism, it was not identified with the teaching traditions in the literary or philosophical disciplines, and its institutional connections were slender and somewhat uncertain. Some of Plato's dialogues were among the standard prose texts that were read in all courses in Greek at the universities and secondary schools of the period, and this accounted for a wide diffusion of his philosophical ideas. In the academies — a new type of institution, half learned society and half literary club, which flourished especially in Italy throughout the century and afterwards — lectures and courses on the so-called philosophy of love, often based on Platonizing poems and always influenced by Plato's *Symposium* and its commentators, were a common feature, especially in Florence, where the memory of Ficino's Academy was never forgotten. Yet Francesco Patrizi's attempts to introduce courses on Platonic philosophy at the universities of Ferrara and Rome were of short duration, and a similar course given for several decades at Pisa was entrusted to scholars who taught Aristotle at the same time and thus were led to compare and to combine Plato with Aristotle, rather than to give him an undivided allegiance.

Nevertheless it would be a mistake to underestimate the importance of sixteenth-century Platonism, or to overlook its almost ubiquitous presence, often combined with humanism or Aristotelianism or other trends or ideas, but always recognizable in its own distinctive physiognomy. In the course of the century, the works of Plato and of the ancient Platonists, and the connected writings attributed to Orpheus and Zoroaster, to Hermes and the Pythagoreans, were all printed and reprinted in the Greek original and in Latin translations, and likewise the writings of the Renaissance Platonists such as Cusanus, Ficino, and Pico were widely read and diffused, and some of this material even found its way into the vernacular languages, especially French and Italian. By that time, this body of literature supplied scholars and readers with the largest and most substantial alternative for, or supplement to, the works of Aristotle and his commentators. No wonder that its impact was felt in many fields and areas of thought and of learning, although it would be difficult, if not impossible, to bring these various facets of Platonism under one common denominator, or to establish very precise relationships among them.

Among the philosophers we find some who would try to combine Plato and Aristotle, like Francesco Verino, Jacopo Mazzoni, and the Frenchman Jacobus Carpentarius, best known for his sinister role during the Massacre of St. Bartholomew. Others professed their undivided allegiance to Plato, like Francesco da Diacceto, Ficino's successor in Florence, and the Spaniard Sebastian Fox Morcillo, and the greatest of all, Francesco Patrizi. Yet the influence of Plato and Platonism extended far beyond the circle of those who wanted to be known as followers of that tradition. The natural philosophers of the time who are best known for their original speculations, like Paracelsus, Telesio, or Bruno, were strongly indebted to the Pla-

tonic tradition. Telesio, who distinguishes between two
souls, is a thorough empiricist when dealing with the lower
soul, to which he assigns our ordinary functions and activities, but follows the Platonists in his treatment of the
higher, immortal soul. And Bruno is a Platonist not only
in his *Heroic Enthusiasts,* where he develops a theory of
love derived from the *Symposium* and its interpreters, but
also in his metaphysics, where he borrows his concept of
the world soul from Plotinus and follows Cusanus on other
important points.[27] (The broad stream of astrological and
alchemical literature, which continued and even increased
during the sixteenth century, also presupposes such notions
as a world soul or the inner powers and affinities of things
celestial, elementary, and composite, notions that go back
to Arabic sources that were still widely used in these circles,
but which derived new impetus and dignity from the Greek
and modern Platonist writers and from the Hermetic works
associated with them.) On the other hand, we note that certain Aristotelian philosophers like Nifo, who wanted to defend the immortality of the soul, made use of the arguments
given in Plato's *Phaedo* or in Ficino's *Platonic Theology,*
and that even the more "naturalistic" among the Renaissance Aristotelians, like Pomponazzi or Cremonini, were
willing to accept certain specific Platonist doctrines. For
the humanists unfriendly to the Aristotelian tradition, Plato
and his school always held much attraction. John Colet
was much impressed by the Areopagite, and we have just
received direct evidence that he was in touch with Marsilio
Ficino.[28] Sir Thomas More translated the life and a few
letters of Pico into English, and his noted *Utopia,* however
original in its content, could hardly have been conceived
without the reading of Plato's *Republic.*[29] Erasmus, in the
Enchiridion and the later part of the *Praise of Folly,* endorsed a somewhat diluted form of Platonism when he opposed the higher folly of the inner spiritual life to the

lower folly of ordinary existence, and Peter Ramus used at least the name of Plato in his bold attempt to replace the traditional Aristotelian logic of the schools. In France, scholars like Lefèvre d'Etaples, Charles de Bouelles, Symphorien Champier, and others received many of their ideas from Cusanus and Ficinus,[30] Pico apparently affected Zwingli,[31] and his Christian cabalism was adopted by Reuchlin and by many other Platonizing theologians.[32] A few scholars have even discovered Platonist elements in the theology of Calvin.[33] Theologians like Ambrosius Flandinus, who opposed both Pomponazzi and Luther, composed commentaries on Plato, or like Aegidius of Viterbo, general of the Augustinian Hermits, wrote a commentary on the *Sentences* "ad mentem Platonis."[34] When the Lateran Council of 1513 condemned Averroes' unity of the intellect and promulgated the immortality of the soul as an official dogma of the Church, we are inclined to see in this event an effect of Renaissance Platonism upon Catholic theology, especially since the Platonist Aegidius of Viterbo endorsed and perhaps inspired the decision, whereas the leading Thomist, Caietanus, opposed it,[35] since he departed on this issue, as on some others, from the position of Aquinas, and held with Pomponazzi that the immortality of the soul could not be demonstrated. Aside from the professional theologians, religious writers and poets like Marguerite of Navarre, the poets of the Lyon circle or Joachim Du Bellay were impressed by the Platonist appeal to contemplation and inner experience.[36] Ficino's notion of Platonic love, that is, of the spiritual love for another human being that is but a disguised love of the soul for God, and some of his other concepts, found favor with such contemporary poets as Lorenzo de' Medici and Girolamo Benivieni, and this Platonizing poetry had among its successors in the sixteenth century Michelangelo and Spenser, besides many minor Italian, French, and English authors in whom the Platonist element is not always easy to distinguish from the common pattern of "Petrarchism."[37] It is not correct to say, as do some scholars, that Dante, Guido Cavalcanti, or Petrarch were poets of Platonic love, but they were thus interpreted by Ficino, Landino, and others, and thus it was possible for their imitators in the sixteenth century to merge their style and imagery with those of the genuine Platonist tradition. Ficino's doctrine of Platonic love was repeated and developed not only in many sonnets and other poems of the sixteenth century, but also in a large body of prose literature which grew up around the literary academies and became fashionable with the reading public: the *trattati d'amore*.[38] These dialogues or treatises discuss in different forms the nature and beneficial effects of spiritual love in the Platonist manner, and also a variety of related Platonist doctrines like the immortality of the soul or the existence and knowledge of the pure Ideas. Among the numerous authors who contributed to this literature and who tended to popularize but also to dilute the teachings of Platonism, we find, besides many now forgotten, such influential writers as Bembo and Castiglione, for whom Platonist philosophy was but a passing fancy, and also a poet like Tasso, whose philosophical prose writings have not yet been sufficiently studied, and such serious philosophers as Francesco da Diacceto, Leone Ebreo, and Francesco Patrizi. Giordano Bruno's *Eroici Furori* also belongs in this tradition, and may be better understood against this background. Finally Plato's doctrine of divine madness as expressed in the *Ion* and *Phaedrus* appealed to many poets and literary critics who would either add this Platonic doctrine to an otherwise Aristotelian system of poetics, or use it as the cornerstone of an anti-Aristotelian theory, as was done by Patrizi.[39]

In the theory of painting and of the other visual arts, which was not yet combined with poetics in a single system of aesthetics, as happened in the eighteenth century,[40] the analogy between the conceptions of the artist and the ideas of the divine creator which appears in Cicero, Seneca, Plotinus, and other Middle and Neoplatonic authors was adopted by Duerer and by many later critics.[41] Moreover, the expression of philosophical ideas of Platonist origin has been discussed and partly established in the iconography of the works of such masters as Botticelli, Raphael, and Michelangelo.[42] If we pass from the visual arts to the theory of music, which in the sixteenth century constituted a separate branch of literature unrelated to poetics or the theory of painting, we notice again that Plato is praised and cited by Francesco Gafurio, by Vincenzo Galileo, the father of the great scientist, and by other musical theorists of the time.[43] The extent of this "musical Platonism" has not been investigated, and its precise links with the philosophical tradition remain to be defined. Yet it is worth noting that Ficino was an enthusiastic amateur in music, and wrote several shorter treatises on musical theory. It is conceivable and even probable that the passages on musical proportions in Plato's *Timaeus*, together with Ficino's extensive commentary on them, made a strong impression on those professional musicians who had a literary education and were familiar with the fame and authority of Plato and his school.

Of even greater interest is the impact of Renaissance Platonism upon the sciences, a subject that has been much debated by recent historians. Again, a distinction must be made between the different sciences, which then as now differed so much in method, subject matter, sources, and traditions. Obviously, the history of technology and engineering would show no traces of Platonist, or for that matter of Aristotelian, influence.[44] In natural history also, where the Aristotelian tradition prevailed, Platonism hardly made itself felt. Yet in medicine, astrological and alchemical theories exercised a good deal of influence during that time, and the medical writings of Ficino, which embodied some of his philosophical and astrological views, were widely read, especially in Germany. Yet the main impact of Platonism, as might be expected, was felt in the mathematical sciences, which had been most cultivated and respected by Plato and his followers.[45] Mathematicians who were concerned with the theoretical and philosophical status of their science, and philosophers who wanted to emphasize the certainty and importance of mathematical knowledge, would be inclined to recur either to the number symbolism of the Pythagoreans that had been associated with Platonism since late antiquity, or to the belief in the nonempirical a priori validity and certainty of mathematical concepts and propositions that goes back to Plato himself and that had been reëmphasized by some, though not by all, representatives of the Platonic tradition. This belief was shared but not emphasized by Plotinus or Ficino, who were more concerned with other features of the Platonic tradition, but it was strongly expressed and applied by Cusanus. (In the sixteenth century when the doctrines of Plato and Aristotle were compared with each other, the superiority of quantitative over qualitative knowledge was considered one of the characteristic points of the Platonic position, and against this background it is quite significant that the Platonist Patrizi emphasized the theoretical priority and superiority of mathematics over physics.[46]) This position had great potentialities at a time when mathematics was rapidly progressing, and when the question arose whether the qualitative physics of the Aristotelian tradition should be replaced by a quantitative physics based on mathematics and in a way reducible to it. Hence there is no wonder that some of the founders of modern physical science should have been attracted by at least this feature of Platonism. In the case of Kepler, no doubt seems possible that his cosmology is rooted in Renaissance Platonism, from which he borrowed not only his mathematical conception of the universe but also his notion of cosmic harmony, and at least in his earlier period, his belief in number symbolism and astrology. To understand the validity of Kepler's laws of planetary motion, the modern student of astronomy does not need to be concerned with his Platonist cosmology. Yet the historian of science will do well to recognize that the positive scientific discoveries of the past were never unrelated to the theoretical and philosophical assumptions of the investigating scientist, whether they were true or false from our point of view, whether consciously expressed or tacitly accepted by him. Even if we want to say that Kepler discovered his laws in spite of, and not on account of, his Platonist cosmology, as historians we cannot be concerned only with those parts of his work and thought that have been accepted as true by later scientists, but we must also understand his errors as well, as an integral part of his scientific and philosophical thought. Otherwise, the history of science becomes nothing but a catalogue of disconnected facts, and a modern version of hagiography.

Whereas Kepler's link with the Platonic tradition has been generally admitted, though frequently regretted, the question of Galileo's Platonism has been a more controversial matter.[47] It has been pointed out that, on account of his known dislike for the Aristotelian tradition, he tended to attribute to Aristotle views which he opposed and which are not always consistent with each other or with the text of Aristotle. It also must be admitted that he borrowed much more from that tradition than one might expect, including such important notions as the distinction between analysis and synthesis in the method of scientific knowledge. His atomism and his distinction between primary and secondary qualities is ultimately derived from Democritus, and his conviction that mathematical relations can be exactly reproduced by material conditions is radically opposed to

Plato. On the other hand, his claims for the absolute certainty of mathematical knowledge are truly Platonic, and his demand that nature should be understood in quantitative, mathematical terms is no less in line with the Platonist position of his time because he rejects the Pythagorean number symbolism often associated with it. Finally, in the famous passage where he also refers to Plato's theory of reminiscence, he states not merely that first principles are evident without demonstration, as any Aristotelian would have granted, but that they are spontaneously known and produced by the human mind, which is specifically Platonic.[48] The fact that there are Aristotelian, Democritean, and novel elements in Galileo's thought does not disprove that Platonic notions are also present in it, and as long as we are inclined to attribute any significance to these latter notions, we are entitled to assign to Galileo a place in the history of Platonism.

With the beginning of a new period of philosophical and scientific thought in the seventeenth century, the Platonic tradition ceases to dominate the development as a separate movement, but continues to influence a number of secondary currents and the thought of many leading thinkers. In the case of Descartes, his indebtedness to scholastic terminology and arguments is now generally admitted, but it has also been shown, though this is less widely known, that he borrowed important elements in ethics from the Stoics, and in epistemology and metaphysics from Platonism.[49] Spinoza's thought contains many Platonist elements, and his notion of the intellectual love of God has been connected with the love speculation of the Renaissance, and especially with Leone Ebreo. It is even easier to point out the Platonizing elements in Malebranche, Leibniz, Kant, and Goethe. Even England, where the prevailing philosophical and scientific tradition seems to be represented by Bacon, Locke, and Hume, by Boyle and Newton, produced in the seventeenth century a group of interesting thinkers, the so-called Cambridge Platonists, who professed their allegiance to Platonism and actually constitute the most important phase of professed Platonism after the Florentine Academy.[50] Thus it is not surprising to find strong Platonizing tendencies in the late Berkeley, in Shaftesbury, and in Coleridge, authors who in turn exercised a rather wide influence.

Thus I hope that it has become apparent that Renaissance Platonism, in spite of its complex and somewhat elusive nature, was an important phenomenon both for its own period and for the subsequent centuries down to 1800. We must resign ourselves to the fact that in most cases the Platonist elements of thought are combined with doctrines of a different origin and character, and that even the professed Platonists did not express the thought of Plato in its purity, as modern scholars understand it, but combined it with more or less similar notions that had accrued to it in late antiquity, the Middle Ages, or more recent times. Yet if we understand Platonism with these qualifications and in a broad and flexible sense, it was a powerful intellectual force throughout the centuries, and we shall understand its nature best if we realize that until the rise of modern Plato scholarship, Plato appealed to his readers not only through the content of his inimitable dialogues, but also through the diverse and often complicated ideas which his commentators and followers down to the sixteenth and seventeenth centuries had associated with him.

4. PAGANISM AND CHRISTIANITY

YOU MIGHT easily raise the question whether the problem which I propose to discuss in this lecture is relevant to the general topic of this series, and there is no doubt that I feel quite unequipped to deal with it appropriately. Yet although philosophical thought has its own distinctive core which ought to be always considered in its own terms, its history in a broader sense can rarely be understood without taking into account the religious as well as the scientific and literary currents of a particular age. In the period which we have been discussing in these lectures, religious events such as the Protestant and Catholic Reformations were of such momentous importance, and their significance in relation to the Renaissance has been the subject of so much debate, that even a short and superficial account of Renaissance thought would be incomplete without some consideration of the Reformation. Some scholars have seemingly avoided this problem by treating the Reformation as a new epoch, different from, and in a sense opposed to, the Renaissance. We prefer to consider the Reformation as an important development within the broader historical period which extended at least to the end of the sixteenth century, and which we continue to call, with certain qualifications, the Renaissance. Obviously, it cannot be our task to describe the original contributions made by the reformers to religious thought, let alone the changes in ecclesiastic institutions brought about by their initiative, or the political and social factors which accounted for their popularity and success. In accordance with our general topic, we shall merely try to understand in which ways, positive or negative, the classicism of the Renaissance exercised an influence upon the religious thought of the period, and especially upon the Reformation.

Many historians of the last century tended to associate the Italian Renaissance and Italian humanism with some kind of irreligion, and to interpret the Protestant and Catholic Reformations as expressions of a religious revival which challenged and finally defeated the un-Christian culture of the preceding period.[1] The moral ideas and literary allegories in the writings of the humanists were taken to be expressions, real or potential, overt or concealed, of a new paganism incompatible with Christianity. The neat separation between reason and faith advocated by the Aristotelian philosophers was considered as a hypocritical device to cover up a secret atheism, whereas the emphasis on a natural religion common to all men, found in the work of the Platonists and Stoics, was characterized as pantheism.[2] This picture of the supposed paganism of the Renaissance which was drawn by historians with much horror or enthusiasm, depending on the strength of their religious or irreligious convictions, can partly be dismissed as the result of later legends and preconceptions. In part, it may be traced to charges made against the humanists and philosophers by hostile or narrow-minded contemporaries, which should not be accepted at their face value.[3] Most recent historians have taken quite a different view of the matter.[4] There was, to be sure, a good deal of talk about the pagan gods and heroes in the literature of the Renaissance, and it was justified by the familiar device of allegory, and strengthened by the belief in astrology, but there were few, if any, thinkers who seriously thought of reviving ancient pagan cults. The word pantheism had not yet been invented,[5] and although the word atheism was generously used in polemics during the later sixteenth century,[6] there were probably few real atheists and barely a few pantheists during the Renaissance. The best or worst we may say is that there were some thinkers who might be considered, or actually were considered, as forerunners of eighteenth-century free thought. There was then, of course, as there was before and afterwards, a certain amount of religious indifference and of merely nominal adherence to the doctrines of the Church. There were many cases of conduct in private and public life that were not in accordance with the moral commands of Christianity, and there were plenty of abuses in ecclesiastic practice itself, but I am not inclined to consider this as distinctive of the Renaissance period.

The real core of the tradition concerning Renaissance paganism is something quite different: it is the steady and irresistible growth of nonreligious intellectual interests which were not so much opposed to the content of religious doctrine, as rather competing with it for individual and public attention. This was nothing fundamentally new, but rather a matter of degree and of emphasis. The Middle Ages was certainly a religious epoch, but it would be wrong to assume that men's entire attention was occupied by religious, let alone by theological, preoccupations. Medieval architects built castles and palaces, not only cathedrals and monasteries. Even when the clerics held the monopoly of learning, they cultivated grammar and the other liberal arts besides theology, and during the High Middle Ages, when specialization began to arise, nonreligious literature also expanded. The thirteenth century produced not Thomas Aquinas alone, as some people seem to believe, or other scholastic theologians, but also a vast literature on Roman law, medicine, Aristotelian logic and physics, mathematics and astronomy, letter-writing and rhetoric, and even on classical Latin poetry, not to mention the chronicles and histories, the lyric and epic poetry in Latin and in the vernacular languages. This development made further progress during the Renaissance period, as a glance at the inventory of a manuscript collection or at a bibliography of printed books will easily reveal, and it continued unchecked during and after the Reformation, whatever the theologians of that time or later times may have felt about it. If an age where the nonreligious concerns that had been growing for centuries attained a kind of equilibrium with religious and theological thought, or even began to surpass it in vitality and appeal, must be called pagan, the Renaissance was pagan, at least in certain places and phases. Yet since the religious convictions of Christianity were either retained or transformed, but never really challenged, it seems more appropriate to call the Renaissance a fundamentally Christian age.

To prove this point, it would be pertinent in the first place to state that the medieval traditions of religious thought and literature continued without interruption until and after the Reformation, and that Italy was no exception to this rule. The study of theology and canon law, and the literary production resulting from it, tended to increase rather than to decline, a fact that is often overlooked because historians of these subjects have paid less attention to that period than to the earlier ones, except for the material directly connected with the Reformation controversies. German mysticism was succeeded during the very period with which we are concerned by the more practical and less speculative *Devotio Moderna* in the Low Countries, a movement that produced such an important document as the *Imitation of Christ,* contributed to a reform of secondary education all over Northern Europe, and had a formative influence on such thinkers as Cusanus and Erasmus.[7] Effective preachers made a deep impression on the learned and unlearned alike all over fifteenth-century Italy, and sometimes led to revivalist movements and political repercussions, of which Savonarola is the most famous but by no means an isolated instance.[8] In Italy no less than in the rest of Europe, the religious guilds directed the activities of the laity and exercised a tremendous influence upon the visual arts, music, and literature.[9] Partly in connection with these guilds, an extensive religious literature of a popular character was circulated, which was composed either by clerics or by laymen, but always addressed to the latter and usually in the vernacular languages. These facts, along with the persistence of church doctrine, institutions, and worship, would go a long way to prove the religious preoccupations of the Renaissance period.

Yet we are not so much concerned with the undoubted survival of medieval Christianity in the Renaissance as with the changes and transformations which affected religious thought during that period. As a distinguished historian has put it,[10] Christianity is not only medieval, but also ancient and modern, and thus it was possible for Christian thought during the Renaissance to cease being medieval in many respects, and yet to remain Christian. This novelty is apparent in the new doctrines and institutions created by the Protestant and Catholic Reformations, a topic on which I shall not attempt to elaborate. I shall merely show that the humanist movement, as we have tried to describe it in our first lecture, had its share in bringing about those changes in religious thought.

The view that the humanist movement was essentially pagan or anti-Christian cannot be sustained. It was successfully refuted by the humanists themselves when they defended their work and program against the charges of unfriendly theologians of their own time. The opposite view, which has had influential defenders in recent years, namely that Renaissance humanism was in its origin a religious movement,[11] or even a religious reaction against certain antireligious tendencies in the Middle Ages,[12] seems to me equally wrong or exaggerated. I am convinced that humanism was in its core neither religious nor antireligious, but a literary and scholarly orientation that could be and, in many cases, was pursued without any explicit discourse on religious topics by individuals who otherwise might be fervent or nominal members of one of the Christian churches. On the other hand, there were many scholars and thinkers with a humanist training who had a genuine concern for religious and theological problems, and it is my contention that the way they brought their humanist training to bear upon the source material and subject matter of Christian theology was one of the factors responsible for the changes which Christianity underwent during that period.[12a] The most important elements in the humanist approach to religion and theology were the attack upon the scholastic method and the emphasis upon the return to the classics, which in this case meant the Christian classics, that is, the Bible and the Church Fathers.

In order to understand the significance of these attitudes, we must once more go back to antiquity and the Middle Ages. Christianity originated in a Jewish Palestine which had become politically a part of the Roman Empire, and culturally a part of the Hellenistic world. At the time when the new religion began to spread through the Mediterranean area, its sacred writings which were to form the canon of the New Testament were composed in Greek, that is, in a language which showed the marks of a long literary and philosophical tradition, and in part by authors such as Paul, Luke, and John, who had enjoyed a literary and perhaps a philosophical education. In the following centuries, the early Apologists, the Greek Fathers, and the great Councils were engaged in the task of defining and developing Christian doctrine, and of making it acceptable to the entire Greek-speaking world. Thus the reading and study of the Greek poets and prose writers was finally approved, with some reservations, whereas the teachings of the Greek philosophical schools were subjected to careful examination, rejecting everything that seemed incompatible with Christian doctrine, but using whatever appeared compatible to bolster and to supplement Christian theology. After the precedent of Philo the Jew, Clement of Alexandria and the other Greek Fathers went a long way in adding Greek philosophical methods and notions, especially Stoic and Platonist, to the doctrinal, historical and institutional teachings contained in the Bible, and in creating out of these diverse elements a novel and coherent Christian view of God, the universe, and man. At the same time, a similar synthesis of ancient and Christian elements was achieved by the Latin Fathers of the Western Church. Writers like Arnobius, Cyprian, Lactantius, and Ambrose embody in their writings the best grammatical and rhetorical training, based on the Roman poets and orators, that was available in their time. Jerome added to his consummate Latin literary education that Greek and Hebrew scholarship which enabled him to translate the entire Bible from the original languages into Latin. Augustine, the most important and complex of them all, was not only an excellent and cultured rhetorician according to the standards of his time, but also made use of the allegorical method to justify the study of the ancient Roman poets and prose writers.[13] Furthermore, Augustine was a learned and productive philosophical and theological thinker, who left to posterity a substantial body of writings in which traditional religious doctrine was enriched with more elaborate theological ideas like the City of God, original sin, and predestination, and also with philosophical conceptions of Greek and especially Neoplatonic origin, like the eternal forms in the divine mind, the incorporeality and immortality of the soul, conceptions which appear more prominently in his earlier, philosophical writings, but which he did not completely abandon even in his later years when he was engaged in Church administration and in theological controversies with the heretics of his time. Thus Christianity, during the first six centuries of its existence, which still belong to the period of classical antiquity, absorbed a large amount of Greek philosophical ideas and of Greek and Latin literary traditions, so that some historians have been able to speak, with a certain amount of justification, of the humanism of the Church Fathers. In recent years, it has become customary among theologians and historians to ignore or to minimize the indebtedness of Philo, Augustine, and the other early Christian writers to Greek philosophy.[14] I must leave it to the judgment of present-day theologians and their followers whether they are really serving their cause by trying to eliminate from Christian theology all notions originally derived from Greek philosophy. Certainly those historians who follow a similar tendency and deny the significance of Greek philosophy for early Christian thought can be corrected through an objective study of the sources.

During the early Middle Ages, the Latin West had very limited philosophical and scientific interests, as we have seen, but it continued as best it could the grammatical and theological studies sanctioned by Augustine and the other Latin Fathers; and a number of Spanish, Irish, Anglo-Saxon and Carolingian scholars achieved distinction in this way. In the history of theology, a marked change from the pattern of the patristic period occurred with the rise of scholasticism after the eleventh century.[15] What was involved was not merely the influx of additional philosophical sources and ideas, both Platonist and Aristotelian, of which we have spoken in the preceding lectures. Much more important was the novel tendency to transform the subject matter of Christian theology into a topically arranged and logically coherent system. There was no precedent for this either in the Bible or in Latin patristic literature, although certain Greek writers like Origen and John of Damascus had paved the way. The desire for a topical arrangement found its expression in the collections of sentences and church canons which culminated in the twelfth century in the *Libri Sententiarum* of Peter Lombard and the *Decretum* of Gratian which for many centuries were to serve as the standard textbooks of theology and of canon law. At the same time, the rising interest in Aristotelian logic led to the endeavor, first cultivated in the schools of Bec, Laon, and Paris, to apply the newly refined methods of dialectical argument to the subject matter of theology, which thus became by the standards of the time a real science. It is this method of Anselm, Abelard, and Peter Lombard which dominates the theological tradition of the high and later Middle Ages, including Bonaventura, Aquinas, Duns Scotus, and Ockham, not the older method of Peter Damiani or St. Bernard, who tried in vain to stem the rising tide of scholasticism and whose influence was hence confined to the more popular and practical, less scientific areas of later religious literature.

If we remember these facts concerning the history of theology in the West, we can understand what it meant for a Renaissance humanist with religious convictions to attack scholastic theology and to advocate a return to the Biblical and patristic sources of Christianity. It meant that these sources, which after all were themselves the product of antiquity, were considered as the Christian classics which shared the prestige and authority of classical antiquity and to which the same methods of historical and philological scholarship could be applied.[16] Thus Petrarch shuns the medieval theologians except St. Bernard and a few other prescholastic writers and quotes only early Christian writers in his religious and theological remarks.[17] Valla laments the harmful influence of logic and philosophy upon theology and advocates an alliance between faith and eloquence. And Erasmus repeatedly attacks the scholastic theologians and emphasizes that the early Christian writers were grammarians, but no dialecticians. In his rejection of scholastic theology and his emphasis on the authority of Scripture and the Fathers, even Luther no less than John Colet is in agreement with the humanists, whereas the attempt to combine the study of theology with an elegant Latin style and a thorough knowledge of the Greek and Latin classics characterizes not only many Italian humanists and Erasmus, but also Melanchthon, Calvin,[18] Hooker, and the early Jesuits.

If we try to assess the positive contributions of humanist scholarship to Renaissance theology, we must emphasize above all their achievements in what we might call sacred philology.[19] Valla led the way with his notes on the New Testament, in which he criticized several passages of Jerome's Vulgate on the basis of the Greek text. He was followed by Manetti, who made a new translation of the New Testament from Greek into Latin and of the Psalms from Hebrew into Latin, a work which has not yet been sufficiently studied.[20] Erasmus' edition of the Greek New Testament is well known. It is this humanist tradition of biblical philology which provides the background and method for Luther's German version of the entire Bible from the Hebrew and Greek, as well as for the official revision of the Vulgate accomplished by Catholic scholars during the second half of the sixteenth century,[21] and for the official English version completed under King James I. The theological exegesis of the Bible and of its various parts had always been an important branch of Christian literature ever since patristic times. It was temporarily overshadowed, though by no means eliminated, by the predominance of Peter Lombard's *Sentences* in the theological curriculum of the later Middle Ages, but it derived new force in the sixteenth century from the emphasis of Protestant theology upon the original source of Christian doctrine. To what extent the exegesis of that period was affected by the new methods and standards of humanist philology, seems to be a question which has not yet been sufficiently investigated.[22]

An even wider field was offered to humanist scholarship by the large body of Greek Christian literature of the patristic and Byzantine period. Some of this material had been translated into Latin towards the end of antiquity and again during the twelfth century. Yet it is an established fact not sufficiently known or appreciated that a large proportion of Greek patristic literature was for the first time translated into Latin by the humanists and humanistically trained theologians of the fifteenth and sixteenth centuries.[23] This applies to many important writings of Eusebius, Basil, and John Chrysostom, of Gregory of Nazianzus and of Nyssa, not to mention many later or lesser authors, or the writings which had been known before and were now reissued in presumably better Latin versions. Early in the fifteenth century, Leonardo Bruni translated Basil's letter which defended the reading of the pagan poets on the part of Christian students, and this welcome support of the humanist program by a distinguished Church author attained a very wide circulation and was even used in the classroom outside of Italy.[24] About the same time, Ambrogio Traversari, a monk with a classical training, dedicated a considerable amount of his energy to the translating of Greek Christian writers, thus setting an example to many later scholars, clerics, and laymen alike. These Latin versions attained great popularity as the numerous manuscript copies and printed editions may prove. They were often followed by vernacular translations, and in the sixteenth century, by editions of the original Greek texts. Thus we must conclude that the Renaissance possessed a much better and more complete knowledge of Greek Christian literature and theology than the preceding age, and it would be an interesting question, which to my knowledge has not yet been explored, whether or to what extent the newly diffused ideas of these Greek authors exercised an influence on the theological discussions and controversies of the Reformation period.

Whereas a considerable proportion of Greek Christian literature was thus made available to the West through the labors of the humanists, the writings of the Latin Church Fathers had been continuously known through the Middle Ages, and never ceased to exercise a strong influence on all theologians and other writers. Yet in this area also humanist scholarship brought about significant changes. The humanists were fully aware of the fact that authors like Ambrose and Lactantius, and especially Jerome and Augustine, belong to the good period of ancient Latin literature, and hence must be considered as "Christian classics." Consequently, some of their works were included in the curriculum of the humanistic school, as in that of Guarino,[25] and regularly listed as recommended readings by humanist educators like Bruni, Valla, Erasmus, and Vives. Thus the Latin Fathers were read in the humanistic period no less than before, but they were grouped with the classical Latin writers rather than with the medieval theologians, and this fact could not fail to bring about a change in the way in which they were read and understood.

Moreover, the new philological methods of editing and commenting which the humanists had developed in their studies of the ancient authors were also applied to the Latin Church Fathers. We know in the case of Augustine that many manuscript copies and printed editions of the fifteenth century were due to the efforts of humanist scholars, and that Vives composed a philological commentary on the City of God, with which he was said in true humanist fashion to have restored St. Augustine to his ancient integrity. The application of humanist scholarship to Latin patristic literature culminated in the work of Erasmus, who prepared for a number of the most important writers critical editions of their collected works. His example was followed by Protestant and Catholic scholars alike, and later in the sixteenth century, the pope appointed a special committee of scholars for the purpose of publishing the writings of the Fathers in new critical editions.[26]

Another field in which humanist scholarship was applied to the problems which concerned the churches and theologians was the study of ecclesiastic history. The critical methods developed by the humanists for the writing of ancient and medieval history on the basis of authentic contemporary documents and evidence were first applied to church history by Valla in his famous attack on the Donation of Constantine. In the sixteenth century, the Magdeburg Centuriatores used this method to rewrite the whole history of the church from the Protestant point of view, and later in the century, Cardinal Baronius and his assistants undertook the same task for the Catholic side.[27]

The humanist interest in early Christian literature was not limited to philological and historical preoccupations, but also had its doctrinal consequences in philosophy and theology. Just as the philological study of the pagan philosophers led the way towards a revival of Platonism and of other ancient philosophies, and more specifically to a new kind of Aristotelianism, so the humanistic study of the Bible and of the Church Fathers led to new interpretations of early Christian thought, that are characteristic of the Renaissance and Reformation period. Thus the attempt to interpret the Epistles of Paul without the context and superstructure of scholastic theology was made by scholars like Ficino, Colet, and Erasmus before it had such powerful and decisive results in the work of Luther.[28] Even more significant and more widespread was the influence exercised during the Renaissance by St. Augustine, and hence I should like to discuss, as briefly as possible, some aspects of Renaissance Augustinianism.[29]

The terms "Augustinianism" or "the Augustinian tradi-

tion" cover almost as many different meanings as the term
"Platonism," since a thinker may be called an Augustinian
for many different reasons. The cause of this ambiguity is
the same as in the case of Plato: the great variety and
complexity of Augustine's work. Before he had become a
bishop and a dogmatic theologian, Augustine had been a
rhetorician, a philosopher, and a heretic who underwent a
conversion, and all these elements and experiences left their
traces in his writings. Augustine is a preacher, a moral
teacher, and a political thinker, an expositor of the Bible,
an autobiographer, a skeptic and neoplatonic philosopher,
a rhetorically trained writer who finds a justification for
the study of the pagan poets, a systematic theologian who
continues the work of the Greek Fathers, a vigorous op-
ponent of heresies who formulated or sharpened the doctrines of original sin, grace, and predestination. All these
elements were potential sources of inspiration for later
readers of Augustine's works.

During the early Middle Ages, Augustine's influence
was chiefly felt in the fields of theology proper, education,
and political thought. During the rise of scholasticism in
the eleventh and twelfth centuries, Augustine's works supplied the chief philosophical and theological inspiration,
and most of the early scholastics have been rightly called
Augustinians. During the thirteenth and fourteenth centuries when Aristotle became predominant among the
philosophers and theologians, Augustinianism survived as
an important secondary current, and even the Aristotelians
preserved many traces of Augustinian influence. At the
same time, the theology of the mystics, and the broad
stream of popular religious literature remained unaffected
by Aristotle and faithful to the spirit of Augustine.

The influence of Augustine during the Renaissance period followed in part the same lines taken during the preceding centuries. The Augustinian current in scholastic

philosophy and theology can be traced through the fifteenth century and afterwards, and the popular religious literature affected by his ideas increased in volume during the same period. Among the leaders of the *Devotio Moderna* in the Low Countries, after the Bible Augustine was the leading authority, as he had been with St. Bernard and the German mystics.

Yet besides these traditional lines of Augustinian influence whose importance should not be underestimated, we also note certain attitudes towards Augustine that seem to be of a different type. For Petrarch, who ignores and dislikes scholastic theology but always emphasizes his religious convictions, Augustine was one of the favorite authors who even exercised a decisive influence upon his spiritual development. Aside from numerous citations, two instances deserve special mention. When Petrarch composed his most personal work, the *Secretum,* he gave it the form of a dialogue between Augustine and the author, and it is Augustine who takes the part of the spiritual guide who resolves the doubts and questions of the poet. And in the famous letter describing his climbing of Mont Ventoux, Petrarch tells us that he took Augustine's *Confessions* out of his pocket, opened them at random, and found a passage which appropriately expressed his own feelings: "Men go to admire the heights of the mountains, the great floods of the sea, the shores of the ocean, and the orbits of the stars, and neglect themselves." Thus it was the Augustine of the *Confessions,* the man who eloquently expresses his feelings and experiences, not the dogmatic theologian, who impressed Petrarch and other later humanists and helped them to reconcile their religious convictions with their literary tastes and personal opinions. Only Erasmus, who had done so much for the text of Augustine, was unsympathetic to his theology and to his interpretation of the Bible, preferring that of St. Jerome, and significantly enough was taken to task for it by Catholics and Protestants alike.

Another strand of Augustinian influence in the Renaissance may be found among the Platonists of the period. Augustine's witness in favor of Plato and the Platonists, already utilized by Petrarch against the authority of Aristotle, was eagerly cited by all philosophers sympathetic to Platonism from Bessarion to Patrizi. At least some of these Platonists also derived important philosophical ideas from the writings of Augustine. Thus Cusanus, who was in many ways affected by the thought of Augustine, took from one of his letters the term "learned ignorance," which he used to describe the characteristic method of his speculation. And Ficino not only states that his allegiance to the Platonic school was partly determined by the authority of Augustine, but also derived from a direct reading of Augustine's works some very essential elements of his philosophy, as a more detailed analysis of his works would easily show. To mention only one example, when Ficino in the preface to his main philosophical work announces his intention of interpreting Plato's philosophy primarily in terms of the soul and of God, he is clearly following the lead of St. Augustine. Yet it is again characteristic that Ficino seems to know Augustine mainly from such well-known works as the *Confessions,* the *City of God,* and the *De Trinitate,* and in addition from those early philosophical and Platonist writings that have been minimized by the theological admirers of the great Church Father, whereas he apparently showed less interest in Augustine's later theological writings.

Very different but no less powerful was the influence which Augustine exercised upon the theological writers, both Protestant and Catholic, of the sixteenth and seventeenth centuries. It was the theology of the later writings of Augustine, with their emphasis on predestination, sin, and grace, which was taken up by Luther and Calvin and their successors, whereas the theologians of the Catholic Reformation, and later the Jansenists and Oratorians, derived very different theological ideas from the interpretation of Augustine's thought. It is true that these theological developments were far removed from the interests and ideas of Renaissance humanism, but it seems reasonable to remember that the authority granted to Augustine, to the other patristic writers, and to Scripture itself has something to do with the humanist emphasis on ancient sources and with their contempt for the medieval tradition of scholastic theology.

I think we are now at last prepared to offer a meaningful interpretation of the term "Christian humanism" that is so often applied to the Renaissance or to earlier periods.[30] Confining the term humanism, according to the Renaissance meaning of the words humanist and humanities, to the rhetorical, classical, and moral concerns of the Renaissance humanists, regardless of the particular philosophical or theological opinions held by individual humanists, and of the theological, philosophical, scientific, or juristic training which individual scholars may have combined with their humanist education, we might choose to call Christian humanists all those scholars who accepted the teachings of Christianity and were members of one of the churches, without necessarily discussing religious or theological topics in their literary or scholarly writings. By this standard, practically all Renaissance humanists, before and after the Reformation, were Christian humanists, since the alleged cases of openly pagan or atheistic convictions are rare and dubious. But it is probably preferable to use the term Christian humanism in a more specific sense, and to limit it to those scholars with a humanist classical and rhetorical training who explicitly discussed religious or theological problems in all or some of their writings. In this sense, neither Aquinas nor Luther were Christian humanists, for the simple reason that they were theologians, but not humanists as that term was then understood, although Luther presupposes certain scholarly achievements of humanism. On the other hand, we must list among the Christian humanists not only Erasmus, Vives, Budé, More and Hooker, but also Calvin, the elegant Latin writer and commentator of Seneca; Melanchthon, the defender of rhetoric against philosophy, who had more influence on many aspects of Lutheran Germany than Luther himself and who was responsible for the humanistic tradition of the German Protestant schools down to the nineteenth century; and finally the Jesuit Fathers, many of whom were excellent classical scholars and Latin writers, and who owed part of their success to the good instruction offered in their schools and colleges in the then fashionable humanistic disciplines. For the tradition of humanist learning by no means came to an end with the Protestant or Catholic Reformations, as might appear if we look only for the headlines of the historical development. It survived as vigorously as did the tradition of Aristotelian scholasticism, cutting across all religious and national divisions, flourishing at Leiden and Oxford no less than at Padua and Salamanca, and exercising as formative an influence upon the minds of the philosophers and scientists trained in the schools and universities of the seventeenth and eighteenth centuries.

We have at last reached the end of our long and rapid journey, and it is time for me to thank you for having kept me company, and to sum up my impressions and recollections. We might state briefly that the period which we call the Renaissance attained a much more accurate and more complete acquaintance with ancient Latin and especially Greek literature than had been possible in the preceding age. And we have tried to show with a few examples taken from the history of philosophy and theology that this acquaintance was not merely a matter of study and

of imitation, but that the ideas embodied in ancient literature served as a ferment and inspiration for the original
thought of the period, and account at least in part for the
intellectual changes which occurred more slowly in the fifteenth and more rapidly in the sixteenth centuries. These
examples could easily be multiplied from the history of
philosophy as well as from all other areas of intellectual
and cultural history.

With the seventeenth century, there begins a new period
in the history of Western science and philosophy, and the
traditions of the Renaissance begin to recede into the background. Beginning about the middle of the sixteenth century, scholars started to be more conscious of their originality, and to notice the progress made by their own time in
comparison with classical antiquity.[31] The invention of
printing and the discovery of America were now emphasized to illustrate this progress, and during the seventeenth
century, the famous battle of the ancients and moderns led
to a clearer distinction between the sciences, in which modern times had by now surpassed the achievements of the
ancients, and the arts, in which the ancients could never be
surpassed though perhaps equaled. Consequently, when a
new wave of classicism arose during the eighteenth century,
it was limited to literature and poetry, to the visual arts, and
to political thought, but omitted the natural sciences in which
the ancients could no longer be considered as masters.

We are now living in a time in which this wave of eighteenth-century classicism has nearly spent its force. Classical scholarship has become a highly specialized tool in the
hands of a few brave experts who have greatly expanded
the knowledge of their predecessors, at least in certain
areas of their discipline, but who have seemed to lose,
through no fault of their own, more and more ground with
the nonspecialists and with the people at large. Those who
are not trained classical philologists now have reason to

envy any medieval century for at least its Latin learning,
and there are many professional educators and many important sectors of public opinion that seem to be completely unaware of the existence, let alone the importance, of
humanistic scholarship. The situation is such that many
responsible scholars are rightly worried. Yet I am inclined
to hope and to expect that the interest in the classics and in
historical learning will be continued and even revived, for
I am firmly convinced of their intrinsic merit, and believe
that it cannot fail to impose itself again, although perhaps
in a form different from the one to which we are accustomed, and more in accordance with the needs and interests
of our time and society. Thus the study of the history of
civilization and the reading of the classical authors in translations perform a useful service in college education. The
wheel of fashion which in modern times seems to have replaced the wheel of fortune that appears so frequently in
the art and literature of the Middle Ages and of the Renaissance, is likely to bring back at some time that taste for
clarity, simplicity, and conciseness in literature and in
thought that has always found its nourishment in the works
of antiquity. The natural desire to overcome the limits of
our parochial outlook in time as well as in place may stimulate the interest in the classics; for they have not only a
direct appeal for our own time, but also hold many clues
for the understanding of medieval and early modern
thought, which contains in turn the direct roots of our own
contemporary world. It is true that each generation has
its own message, and each individual may make his own
original contribution. The effect of the classics upon Renaissance thought and literature may show us that it is possible to learn from the past and to be original at the same
time. Originality is greatly to be admired, but it is a gift
of nature or providence; it cannot be taught, and I doubt
that it is harmed by knowledge or increased by ignorance.

I do not wish to give the impression that I want to elevate the ideal of scholarship at the expense of other more fundamental and more comprehensive ideals, or that I ignore the limitations of historical learning. We all are, or want to be, not merely scholars, but citizens, persons who work, persons who think, if not philosophers, and human beings. Historical knowledge, as Jacob Burckhardt said, does not make us shrewder for the next time, but wiser forever.[32] It gives us perspective, but it does not give us answers or solutions to the moral, social, or intellectual problems which we face. No amount of information will relieve us of the choices in judgment and in action which we are compelled to make every day. There are unique feelings and experiences in every person's external and spiritual life that have never, or rarely and imperfectly, been expressed by the thinkers and writers of the past. The world of Western civilization, wide and rich in comparison with our present time and society which is but a part of it, is itself small and limited when compared with the entire history of mankind, with the existence of animals, of plants, and of silent nature on our planet, or with the huge, if not infinite, extent in space and time of our visible universe. Exclusive concern for historical scholarship may isolate us from all those persons who for geographical, social or educational reasons cannot participate in it and who as human beings yet demand our sympathetic understanding. Finally, the record of the past in which all battles are decided and many pains forgotten, whereas the most distinguished characters, actions, and works stand out more clearly and in a more final form than they did in their own time, may lull us into a false security and indolence in view of the pains we have to suffer, the decisions we have to make, the actions and works we have to accomplish, without yet knowing the outcome, or the value they may have if and when they appear in turn as a settled and hardened past to a future observer. All these objections and doubts are true, and should be always remembered.   Nevertheless, I hope you will accept with patience this plea for classical scholarship and historical knowledge, since it comes from a person who is not a member of the guild of philologists or historians, and allow me to conclude with a word of Erasmus which he gave as a reply to those theologians who criticized his ideal of scholarship, and which we might easily adapt to our somewhat different situation: "Prayer, to be sure, is the stronger weapon (in our fight against vice) . . . yet knowledge is no less necessary."[33]

5. HUMANISM AND SCHOLASTICISM
IN THE ITALIAN RENAISSANCE

EVER since 1860, when Jacob Burckhardt first published his famous book on the civilization of the Renaissance in Italy,[1] there has been a controversy among historians as to the meaning and significance of the Italian Renaissance.[2] Almost every scholar who has taken part in the discussion felt it was his duty to advance a new and different theory. This variety of views was partly due to the emphasis given by individual scholars to different historical personalities or currents or to different aspects and developments of the Italian Renaissance. Yet the chief cause of the entire Renaissance controversy, at least in its more recent phases, has been the considerable progress made during the last few decades in the field of medieval studies. The Middle Ages are no longer considered as a period of darkness, and consequently many scholars do not see the need for such new light and revival as the very name of the Renaissance would seem to suggest. Thus certain medievalists have questioned the very existence of the Renaissance and would like to banish the term entirely from the vocabulary of historians.

In the face of this powerful attack, Renaissance scholars have assumed a new line of defense. They have shown that the notion embodied in the term *Renaissance* was not an invention of enthusiastic historians of the last century, but was commonly expressed in the literature of the period of the Renaissance itself. The humanists themselves speak continually of the revival or rebirth of the arts and of learning that was accomplished in their own time after a long period of decay.[3] It may be objected that occasional claims of an intellectual revival are also found in medieval literature.[4] Yet the fact remains that during the Renaissance scholars and writers talked of such a revival and rebirth more persistently than at any other period of European history. Even if we were convinced that it was an empty claim and that the humanists did not bring about a real Renaissance, we would still be forced to admit that the illusion itself was characteristic of that period and that the term Renaissance thus had at least a subjective meaning.

Without questioning the validity of this argument, I think that there are also some more objective reasons for defending the existence and the importance of the Renaissance. The concept of style as it has been so successfully applied by historians of art[5] might be more widely applied in other fields of intellectual history and might thus enable us to recognize the significant changes brought about by the Renaissance, without obliging us to despise the Middle Ages or to minimize the debt of the Renaissance to the medieval tradition.

Moreover, I should like to reexamine the relation between the Middle Ages and the Renaissance in the light of the following consideration. Scholars have become so accustomed to stress the universalism of the medieval church and of medieval culture and also to consider the Italian Renaissance as a European phenomenon, that they are apt to forget that profound regional differences existed even during the Middle Ages. The center of medieval civilization was undoubtedly France, and all other countries of Western Europe followed the leadership of that country, from Carolingian times down to the beginning of the fourteenth century.[6] Italy certainly was no exception to that rule; but whereas the other countries, especially England, Germany, and the Low Countries, took an active part in the major cultural pursuits of the period and followed the same general development, Italy occupied a somewhat peculiar position.[7] Prior to the thirteenth century, her active participation in many important aspects of medieval culture lagged far behind that of the other countries. This may be observed in architecture

and music, in the religious drama as well as in Latin and
vernacular poetry in general,[8] in scholastic philosophy and
theology,[9] and even, contrary to common opinion, in classical
studies.   On the other hand, Italy had a narrow but persistent tradition of her own which went back to ancient
Roman times and which found its expression in certain
branches of the arts and of poetry, in lay education and in
legal customs, and in the study of grammar and of rhetoric.[10]
Italy was more directly and more continually exposed to
Byzantine influences than any other Western European country.   Finally, after the eleventh century, Italy developed a
new life of her own which found expression in her trade and
economy, in the political institutions of her cities, in the study
of civil and canon law and of medicine, and in the techniques
of letter-writing and of secular eloquence.[11]   Influences from
France became more powerful only with the thirteenth century, when their traces appeared in architecture and music, in
Latin and vernacular poetry, in philosophy and theology,
and in the field of classical studies.[12]   Many typical products
of the Italian Renaissance may thus be understood as a result of belated medieval influences received from France, but
grafted upon, and assimilated by, a more narrow, but stubborn and different native tradition.   This may be said of
Dante's *Divine Comedy,* of the religious drama which flourished in fifteenth century Florence, and of the chivalric
poetry of Ariosto and of Tasso.

A similar development may be noticed in the history of
learning.   The Italian Renaissance thus should be viewed
not only in its contrast with the French Middle Ages, but
also in its relation to the Italian Middle Ages.   The rich
civilization of Renaissance Italy did not spring directly from
the equally rich civilization of medieval France, but from
the much more modest traditions of medieval Italy.   It is
only about the beginning of the fourteenth century that Italy
witnessed a tremendous increase in all her cultural activities,

and this enabled her, for a certain period, to wrest from France her cultural leadership in Western Europe. Consequently, there can be no doubt that there was an Italian Renaissance, that is, a cultural Renaissance of Italy, not so much in contrast with the Middle Ages in general or with the French Middle Ages, but very definitely in contrast with the Italian Middle Ages. It appears from a letter of Boccaccio that this general development was well understood by some Italians of that period,[13] and we should keep this development constantly in mind if we want to understand the history of learning during the Italian Renaissance.

The most characteristic and most pervasive aspect of the Italian Renaissance in the field of learning is the humanistic movement. I need hardly say that the term "humanism," when applied to the Italian Renaissance, does not imply all the vague and confused notions that are now commonly associated with it. Only a few traces of these may be found in the Renaissance. By humanism we mean merely the general tendency of the age to attach the greatest importance to classical studies, and to consider classical antiquity as the common standard and model by which to guide all cultural activities. It will be our task to understand the meaning and origin of this humanistic movement which is commonly associated with the name of Petrarch.

Among modern historians we encounter mainly two interpretations of Italian humanism. The first interpretation considers the humanistic movement merely as the rise of classical scholarship accomplished during the period of the Renaissance. This view which has been held by most historians of classical scholarship is not very popular at present. The revival of classical studies certainly does not impress an age such as ours which has practically abandoned classical education, and it is easy to praise the classical learning of the Middle Ages, in a time which, except for a tiny number of specialists, knows much less of classical antiquity than did the Middle Ages. Moreover, in a period such as the present, which has much less regard for learning than for practical achievements and for "creative" writing and "original" thinking, a mere change of orientation, or even an increase of knowledge, in the field of learning does not seem to possess any historical significance. However, the situation in the Renaissance was quite different, and the increase in, and emphasis on, classical learning had a tremendous importance.

There are indeed several historical facts which support the interpretation of the humanistic movement as a rise in classical scholarship. The humanists were classical scholars and contributed to the rise of classical studies.[14] In the field of Latin studies, they rediscovered a number of important texts that had been hardly read during the Middle Ages.[15] Also in the case of Latin authors commonly known during the Middle Ages, the humanists made them better known, through their numerous manuscript copies[16] and printed editions, through their grammatical and antiquarian studies, through their commentaries, and through the development and application of philological and historical criticism.

Even more striking was the impulse given by the humanists to the study of Greek. In spite of the political, commercial, and ecclesiastic relations with the Byzantine Empire, during the Middle Ages the number of persons in Western Europe who knew the Greek language was comparatively small, and practically none of them was interested in, or familiar with, Greek classical literature. There was almost no teaching of Greek in Western schools and universities, and almost no Greek manuscripts in Western libraries.[17] In the twelfth and thirteenth centuries, a great number of Greek texts were translated into Latin, either directly or through intermediary Arabic translations, but this activity was almost entirely confined to the fields of mathematics, astronomy, astrology, medicine, and Aristotelian philosophy.[18]

During the Renaissance, this situation rapidly changed. The study of Greek classical literature which had been cultivated in the Byzantine Empire throughout the later Middle Ages, after the middle of the fourteenth century began to spread in the West, both through Byzantine scholars who went to Western Europe for a temporary or permanent stay, and through Italian scholars who went to Constantinople in quest of Greek classical learning.[19] As a result, Greek language and literature acquired a recognized place in the curriculum of Western schools and universities, a place which they did not lose until the present century. A large number of Greek manuscripts was brought from the East to Western libraries, and these manuscripts have formed the basis of most of our editions of the Greek classics. At a later stage, the humanists published printed editions of Greek authors, wrote commentaries on them, and extended their antiquarian and grammatical studies as well as their methods of philological and historical criticism to Greek literature.

No less important, although now less appreciated, were the numerous Latin translations from the Greek due to the humanists of the Renaissance. Almost the whole of Greek poetry, oratory, historiography, theology, and non-Aristotelian philosophy was thus translated for the first time, whereas the medieval translations of Aristotle and of Greek scientific writers were replaced by new humanistic translations. These Latin translations of the Renaissance were the basis for most of the vernacular translations of the Greek classics, and they were much more widely read than were the original Greek texts. For in spite of its remarkable increase, the study of Greek even in the Renaissance never attained the same general importance as did the study of Latin which was rooted in the medieval tradition of the

West. Nevertheless, it remains a remarkable fact that the
study of the Greek classics was taken over by the humanists
of Western Europe at the very time when it was affected in
the East by the decline and fall of the Byzantine Empire.

If we care to remember these impressive facts, we certainly cannot deny that the Italian humanists were the ancestors of modern philologists and historians. Even a
historian of science can afford to despise them only if he
chooses to remember that science is the subject of his study,
but to forget that the method he is applying to this subject
is that of history. However, the activity of the Italian
humanists was not limited to classical scholarship, and hence
the theory which interprets the humanistic movement merely
as a rise in classical scholarship is not altogether satisfactory.
This theory fails to explain the ideal of eloquence persistently
set forth in the writings of the humanists, and it fails to
account for the enormous literature of treatises, of letters,
of speeches, and of poems produced by the humanists.[20]

These writings are far more numerous than the contributions of the humanists to classical scholarship, and they
cannot be explained as a necessary consequence of their
classical studies. A modern classical scholar is not supposed
to write a Latin poem in praise of his city, to welcome a
distinguished foreign visitor with a Latin speech, or to write
a political manifesto for his government. This aspect of
the activity of the humanists is often dismissed with a slight-
ing remark about their vanity or their fancy for speech-making. I do not deny that they were vain and loved to make
speeches, but I am inclined to offer a different explanation
for this side of their activity. The humanists were not
classical scholars who for personal reasons had a craving
for eloquence, but, vice versa, they were professional rhetoricians, heirs and successors of the medieval rhetoricians,[21]
who developed the belief, then new and modern, that the

best way to achieve eloquence was to imitate classical models, and who thus were driven to study the classics and to found classical philology. Their rhetorical ideals and achievements may not correspond to our taste, but they were the starting point and moving force of their activity, and their classical learning was incidental to it.

The other current interpretation of Italian humanism, which is prevalent among historians of philosophy and also accepted by many other scholars, is more ambitious, but in my opinion less sound. This interpretation considers humanism as the new philosophy of the Renaissance, which arose in opposition to scholasticism, the old philosophy of the Middle Ages.[22] Of course, there is the well known fact that several famous humanists, such as Petrarch, Valla, Erasmus, and Vives, were violent critics of medieval learning and tended to replace it by classical learning. Moreover, the humanists certainly had ideals of learning, education, and life that differed from medieval modes of thinking. They wrote treatises on moral, educational, political, and religious questions which in tone and content differ from the average medieval treatises on similar subjects. Yet this interpretation of humanism as a new philosophy fails to account for a number of obvious facts. On one hand, we notice a stubborn survival of scholastic philosophy throughout the Italian Renaissance, an inconvenient fact that is usually explained by the intellectual inertia of the respective philosophers whom almost nobody has read for centuries and whose number, problems and literary production are entirely unknown to most historians. On the other, most of the works of the humanists have nothing to do with philosophy even in the vaguest possible sense of the term. Even their treatises on philosophical subjects, if we care to read them, appear in most cases rather superficial and inconclusive if compared with the works of ancient or medieval philosophers, a fact that may be indifferent to a general historian, but which cannot be overlooked by a historian of philosophy.

I think there has been a tendency, in the light of later developments, and under the influence of a modern aversion to scholasticism, to exaggerate the opposition of the humanists to scholasticism, and to assign to them an importance in the history of scientific and philosophical thought which they neither could nor did attain. The reaction against this tendency has been inevitable, but it has been equally wrong. Those scholars who read the treatises of the humanists and noticed their comparative emptiness of scientific and philosophical thought came to the conclusion that the humanists were bad scientists and philosophers who did not live up to their own claims or to those of their modern advocates. I should like to suggest that the Italian humanists on the whole were neither good nor bad philosophers, but no philosophers at all.[22a]

The humanistic movement did not originate in the field of philosophical or scientific studies, but it arose in that of grammatical and rhetorical studies.[22b] The humanists continued the medieval tradition in these fields, as represented, for example, by the *ars dictaminis* and the *ars arengandi,* but they gave it a new direction toward classical standards and classical studies, possibly under the impact of influences received from France after the middle of the thirteenth century. This new development of the field was followed by an enormous growth, both in the quantity and in the quality, of its teaching and its literary production. As a result of this growth, the claims of the humanists for their field of study also increased considerably. They claimed, and temporarily attained, a decided predominance of their field in elementary and secondary education, and a much larger share for it in professional and university education. This development in the field of grammatical and rhetorical studies finally affected the other branches of learning, but it did not displace them. After the middle of the fifteenth century, we find an increasing number of professional jurists, physicians, mathematicians, philosophers, and theologians who cultivated humanistic studies along with their own particular fields of study. Consequently, a humanistic influence began to appear in all these other sciences. It appears in the studied elegance of literary expression, in the increasing use made of classical source materials, in the greater knowledge of history and of critical methods, and also sometimes in an emphasis on new problems. This influence of humanism on the other sciences certainly was important, but it did not affect the content or substance of the medieval traditions in those sciences. For the humanists, being amateurs in those other fields, had nothing to offer that could replace their traditional content and subject matter.

The humanist criticism of medieval science is often sweeping, but it does not touch its specific problems and subject-matter. Their main charges are against the bad Latin style of the medieval authors, against their ignorance of ancient history and literature, and against their concern for supposedly useless questions. On the other hand, even those professional scientists who were most profoundly influenced by humanism did not sacrifice the medieval tradition of their field. It is highly significant that Pico, a representative of humanist philosophy, and Alciato, a representative of humanist jurisprudence, found it necessary to defend their medieval predecessors against the criticism of humanist rhetoricians.[23]

Yet if the humanists were amateurs in jurisprudence, theology, medicine, and also in philosophy, they were themselves professionals in a number of other fields. Their domains were the fields of grammar, rhetoric, poetry, history, and the study of the Greek and Latin authors. They also expanded into the field of moral philosophy, and they made some attempts to invade the field of logic, which were chiefly attempts to reduce logic to rhetoric.[24]

Yet they did not make any direct contributions to the other branches of philosophy or of science. Moreover, much of the humanist polemic against medieval science was not even intended as a criticism of the contents or methods of that science, but merely represents a phase in the "battle of the arts," that is, a noisy advertisement for the field of learning advocated by the humanists, in order to neutralize and to overcome the claims of other, rivaling sciences.[25] Hence I am inclined to consider the humanists not as philosophers with a curious lack of philosophical ideas and a curious fancy for eloquence and for classical studies, but rather as professional rhetoricians with a new, classicist ideal of culture, who tried to assert the importance of their field of learning and to impose their standards upon the other fields of learning and of science, including philosophy.

Let us try to illustrate this outline with a few more specific facts. When we inquire of the humanists, it is often asserted that they were free-lance writers who came to form an entirely new class in Renaissance society.[26] This statement is valid, although with some qualification, for a very small number of outstanding humanists like Petrarch, Boccaccio, and Erasmus. However, these are exceptions, and the vast majority of humanists exercised either of two professions, and sometimes both of them. They were either secretaries of princes or cities, or they were teachers of grammar and rhetoric at universities or at secondary schools.[27] The opinion so often repeated by historians that the humanistic movement originated outside the schools and universities is a myth which cannot be supported by factual evidence. Moreover, as chancellors and as teachers, the humanists, far from representing a new class, were the professional heirs and successors of the medieval rhetoricians, the so-called *dictatores,* who also made their career exactly in these same two professions. The humanist Coluccio Salutati occupied exactly the same place in the society and culture of his time as did the *dictator* Petrus de Vineis one hundred and fifty years before.[28] Nevertheless there was a significant difference between them. The style of writing used by Salutati is quite different from that of Petrus de Vineis or of Rolandinus Passagerii. Moreover, the study and imitation of the classics which was of little or no importance to the medieval *dictatores* has become the major concern for Salutati. Finally, whereas the medieval *dictatores* attained considerable importance in politics and in administration, the humanists, through their classical learning, acquired for their class a much greater cultural and social prestige. Thus the humanists did not invent a new field of learning or a new professional activity, but they introduced a new, classicist style into the traditions of medieval Italian rhetoric. To blame them for not having invented rhetorical studies would be like blaming Giotto for not having been the inventor of painting.

The same result is confirmed by an examination of the literary production of the humanists if we try to trace the medieval antecedents of the types of literature cultivated by the humanists.[29] If we leave aside the editions and translations of the humanists, their classical interests are chiefly represented by their numerous commentaries on ancient authors and by a number of antiquarian and miscellaneous treatises. Theoretical works on grammar and rhetoric, mostly composed for the school, are quite frequent, and even more numerous is the literature of humanist historiography. Dialogues and treatises on questions of moral philosophy, education, politics, and religion have attracted most of the attention of modern historians, but represent a comparatively small proportion of humanistic literature. By far the largest part of that literature, although relatively neglected and partly unpublished, consists of the poems, the speeches, and the letters of the humanists.

If we look for the medieval antecedents of these various

types of humanistic literature, we are led back in many cases to the Italian grammarians and rhetoricians of the later Middle Ages. This is most obvious for the theoretical treatises on grammar and rhetoric.[30] Less generally recognized, but almost equally obvious is the link between humanist epistolography and medieval *ars dictaminis*. The style of writing is different, to be sure, and the medieval term *dictamen* was no longer used during the Renaissance, yet the literary and political function of the letter was basically the same, and the ability to write a correct and elegant Latin letter was still a major aim of school instruction in the Renaissance as it had been in the Middle Ages.[31]

The same link between humanists and medieval Italian rhetoricians which we notice in the field of epistolography may be found also in the field of oratory. Most historians of rhetoric give the impression that medieval rhetoric was exclusively concerned with letter-writing and preaching, represented by the *ars dictaminis* and the somewhat younger *ars praedicandi,* and that there was no secular eloquence in the Middle Ages.[32] On the other hand, most historians of Renaissance humanism believe that the large output of humanist oratory, although of a somewhat dubious value, was an innovation of the Renaissance due to the effort of the humanists to revive ancient oratory and also to their vain fancy for speech-making .[33] Only in recent years have a few scholars begun to realize that there was a considerable amount of secular eloquence in the Middle Ages, especially in Italy.[34] I do not hesitate to conclude that the eloquence of the humanists was the continuation of the medieval *ars arengandi* just as their epistolography continued the tradition of the *ars dictaminis*. It is true, in taking up a type of literary production developed by their medieval predecessors, the humanists modified its style according to their own taste and classicist standards. Yet the practice of speech-making was no invention of the humanists, of course, since it is hardly absent from any human society, and since in medieval Italy it can be traced back at least to the eleventh century.[35]

Even the theory of secular speech, represented by rules and instructions as well as by model speeches, appears in Italy at least as early as the thirteenth century. Indeed practically all types of humanist oratory have their antecedents in this medieval literature: wedding and funeral speeches, academic speeches, political speeches by officials or ambassadors, decorative speeches on solemn occasions, and finally judicial speeches.[36] Some of these types, to be sure, had their classical models, but others, for example, academic speeches delivered at the beginning of the year or of a particular course or upon conferring or receiving a degree, had no classical antecedents whatsoever, and all these types of oratory were rooted in very specific customs and institutions of medieval Italy. The humanists invented hardly any of these types of speech, but they merely applied their standards of style and elegance to a previously existing form of literary expression and thus satisfied a demand, both practical and artistic, of the society of their time. Modern scholars are apt to speak contemptuously of this humanistic oratory, denouncing its empty rhetoric and its lack of "deep thoughts." Yet the humanists merely intended to speak well, according to their taste and to the occasion, and it still remains to be seen whether they were less successful in that respect than their medieval predecessors or their modern successors. Being pieces of "empty rhetoric," their speeches provide us with an amazing amount of information about the personal and intellectual life of their time.

In their historiography, the humanists succeeded the medieval chroniclers, yet they differ from them both in their merits and in their deficiencies.[37] Humanist historiography is characterized by the rhetorical concern for elegant Latin and by the application of philological criticism to the source materials of history. In both respects, they are the predeces-

sors of modern historians.[38] To combine the requirements
of a good style and those of careful research was as rare
and difficult then as it is at present. However, the link
between history and rhetoric that seems to be so typical of
the Renaissance was apparently a medieval heritage. Not
only was the teaching of history in the medieval schools subordinate to that of grammar and rhetoric, but we also find
quite a few medieval historiographers and chronists who
were professional grammarians and rhetoricians.[39] Even
the Renaissance custom of princes and cities appointing official historiographers to write their history seems to have
had a few antecedents in medieval Italy.[40]

Most of the philosophical treatises and dialogues of the
humanists are really nothing but moral tracts, and many of
them deal with subject matters also treated in the moralistic
literature of the Middle Ages. There are, to be sure, significant differences in style, treatment, sources, and solutions.
However, the common features of the topics and literary
patterns should not be overlooked either. A thorough comparative study of medieval and Renaissance moral treatises
has not yet been made so far as I am aware, but in a few
specific cases the connection has been pointed out.[41] Again
it should be added that the very link between rhetoric and
moral philosophy which became so apparent in the Renaissance had its antecedents in the Middle Ages. Medieval
rhetoric, no less than ancient rhetoric, was continually quot-
ing and inculcating moral sentences that interested the authors and their readers for the content as well as for their
form. Moreover, there are at least a few cases in which
medieval rhetoricians wrote treatises on topics of moral
philosophy, or argued about the same moral questions that
were to exercise the minds and pens of their successors, the
Renaissance humanists.[42]

Less definite is the link between humanists and medieval
Italian rhetoricians in the field of Latin poetry. On the

basis of available evidence, it would seem that in the Italian schools up to the thirteenth century verse-making was less cultivated than in France. Throughout the earlier Middle Ages, historical and panegyric epics as well as verse epitaphs were composed abundantly in Italy, yet prior to the thirteenth century her share in rhythmical and in didactic poetry seems to have been rather modest.[43] It is only after the middle of the thirteenth century that we notice a marked increase in the production of Latin poetry in Italy, and the appearance of the teaching of poetry in the schools and universities. This development coincides with the earliest traces of Italian humanism, and it is tempting to ascribe it to French influences.[44]

The same may be said with more confidence of the literature of commentaries on the Latin classics, which are the direct result of school teaching. It is often asserted that, Italy throughout the Middle Ages was closer to the classical tradition than any other European country. Yet if we try to trace the type of the humanistic commentary back into the Middle Ages, we find hardly any commentary on a Latin poet or prose writer composed in Italy prior to the second half of the thirteenth century, whereas we find many such commentaries, from the ninth century on, written in France or in the other Western countries that followed the French development.[45] Only after 1300, that is, after the earliest phase of humanism, did Italy produce an increasing number of such commentaries. Also of antiquarian studies there is very little evidence in Italy prior to the latter part of the thirteenth century.[46] Whereas we have abundant information about the reading of the Latin poets and prose writers in the medieval schools of France and of other Western countries, and whereas such centers as Chartres and Orléans in the twelfth and early thirteenth centuries owed much of their fame to the study of the Latin classics,[47] the sources for Italy are silent during the same period and begin to speak only after the middle of the thirteenth century.[48] It was only after the beginning of the fourteenth century that the teaching of poetry and of the classical authors became firmly established in the Italian schools and universities, to continue without interruption throughout the Renaissance.[49] Italian libraries, with the one exception of Monte Cassino, were not so well furnished with Latin classical poets as were some French and German libraries, and it has been noticed that the humanists of the fifteenth century made most of their manuscript discoveries not in Italy, but in other countries. The conclusion seems inevitable that the study of classical Latin authors was comparatively neglected in Italy during the earlier Middle Ages and was introduced from France after the middle of the thirteenth century.[50] The Italian humanists thus took up the work of their medieval French predecessors just about the time when classical studies began to decline in France, and whereas the classical scholarship of the earliest humanists in its range and method was still close to the medieval tradition, that of the later Renaissance developed far beyond anything attained during the Middle Ages. Consequently, if we consider the entire literary production of the Italian humanists we are led to the conclusion that the humanistic movement seems to have originated from a fusion between the novel interest in classical studies imported from France toward the end of the thirteenth century and the much earlier traditions of medieval Italian rhetoric.

We have seen that the humanists did not live outside the schools and universities, but were closely connected with them. The chairs commonly held by the humanists were those of grammar and rhetoric,[51] that is, the same that had been occupied by their medieval predecessors, the *dictatores*. Thus it is in the history of the universities and schools and of their chairs that the connection of the humanists with medieval rhetoric becomes most apparent. However, under the influence of humanism, these chairs underwent a change which affected their name as well as their content and pretenses. About the beginning of the fourteenth century poetry appears as a special teaching subject at Italian universities. After that time, the teaching of grammar was considered primarily as the task of elementary instructors, whereas the humanists proper held the more advanced chairs of poetry and of eloquence. For eloquence was the equivalent of prose writing as well as of speech. The teaching of poetry and of eloquence was theoretical and practical at the same time, for the humanist professor instructed his pupils in verse-making and in speech-making both through rules and through models. Since classical Latin authors were considered as the chief models for imitation, the reading of these authors was inseparably connected with the theoretical and practical teaching of poetry and of eloquence.

Thus we may understand why the humanists of the fourteenth and fifteenth centuries chose to call their field of study poetry and why they were often styled poets even though they composed no works that would qualify them as poets in the modern sense.[52] Also the coronation of poets in the Renaissance must be understood against this background.[53] It had been originally understood as a kind of academic degree, and it was granted not merely for original poetic compositions, but also for the competent study of classical poets.[54]

History was not taught as a separate subject, but formed a part of the study of rhetoric and poetry since the ancient historians were among the prose writers commonly studied in school. Moral philosophy was always the subject of a separate chair and was commonly studied from the *Ethics* and *Politics* of Aristotle. However, after the beginning of the fifteenth century, the chair of moral philosophy was often held by the humanists, usually in combination with that of rhetoric and poetry.[55] This combination reflects the expansion of humanistic learning into the field of moral philosophy. The chairs of Greek language and literature which were an innovation of the fourteenth century were also commonly held by humanists. This teaching was not as closely tied up with the practical concern for writing verses, speeches, or letters as was the study of Latin, and it was therefore more strictly scholarly and philological. On the other hand, since the fifteenth century we find several cases where humanist teachers of Greek offered courses on Greek texts of philosophy and science and thus invaded the territory of the rivaling fields.[56]

Later on the fields of study cultivated by the humanists were given a new and even more ambitious name. Taking up certain expressions found in Cicero and Gellius, the humanists as early as the fourteenth century began to call their field of learning the humane studies or the studies befitting a human being (*studia humanitatis, studia humaniora*).[57] The new name certainly implies a new claim and program, but it covered a content that had existed long before and that had been designated by the more modest names of grammar, rhetoric, and poetry. Although some modern scholars were not aware of this fact, the humanists certainly were, and we have several contemporary testimonies showing that the *studia humanitatis* were considered as the equivalent of grammar, rhetoric, poetry, history, and moral philosophy.[58]

These statements also prove another point that has been confused by most modern historians: the humanists, at least in Italy or before the sixteenth century, did not claim that they were substituting a new encyclopaedia of learning for the medieval one,[59] and they were aware of the fact that their field of study occupied a well defined and limited place within the system of contemporary learning.[60] To be sure, they tended to emphasize the importance of their field in comparison with the other sciences and to encroach upon the latter's territory, but on the whole they did not deny the existence or validity of these other sciences. This well defined place of the *studia humanitatis* is reflected in the new term *humanista* which apparently was coined during the latter half of the fifteenth century and became increasingly popular during the sixteenth century. The term seems to have originated in the slang of university students and gradually penetrated into official usage.[61] It was coined after the model of such medieval terms as *legista, jurista, canonista,* and *artista,* and it designated the professional teacher of the *studia humanitatis.* The term *humanista* in this limited sense thus was coined during the Renaissance, whereas the term *humanism* was first used by nineteenth century historians.[61a] If I am not mistaken, the new term *humanism* reflects the modern and false conception that Renaissance humanism was a basically new philosophical movement, and under the influence of this notion the old term humanist has also been misunderstood as designating the representative of a new *Weltanschauung.* The old term *humanista,* on the other hand, reflects the more modest, but correct, contemporary view that the humanists were the teachers and representatives of a certain branch of learning which at that time was expanding and in vogue, but well limited in its subject matter. Humanism thus did not represent the sum total of learning in the Italian Renaissance.

If we care to look beyond the field of the humanities into the other fields of learning as they were cultivated during the Italian Renaissance, that is, into jurisprudence, medicine, theology, mathematics, and natural philosophy, what we find is evidently a continuation of medieval learning and may hence very well be called scholasticism. Since the term has been subject to controversy, I should like to say that I do not attach any unfavorable connotation to the term scholasticism. As its characteristic, I do not consider any particular doctrine, but rather a specific method, that is, the type of logical argument represented by the form of the *Questio*. It is well known that the content of scholastic philosophy, since the thirteenth century, was largely based on the writings of Aristotle, and that the development of this philosophy, since the twelfth century, was closely connected with the schools and universities of France and England, especially with the universities of Paris and of Oxford. The place of Italy is, however, less known in the history and development of scholastic philosophy. Several Italians are found among the most famous philosophers and theologians of the twelfth and thirteenth centuries, but practically all of them did their studying and teaching in France. Whereas Italy had flourishing schools of rhetoric, of jurisprudence, and of medicine during the twelfth and early thirteenth century, she had no native center of philosophical studies during the same period. After 1220 the new mendicant orders established schools of theology and philosophy in many Italian cities, but unlike those in France and England, these schools of the friars for a long time had no links with the Italian universities. Regular faculties of theology were not established at the Italian universities before the middle of the fourteenth century, and even after that period, the university teaching of theology continued to be spotty and irregular.

Aristotelian philosophy, although not entirely unknown at Salerno toward the end of the twelfth century, made its regular appearance at the Italian universities after the middle of the thirteenth century and in close connection with the teaching of medicine.[62] I think it is safe to assume that Aristotelian philosophy was then imported from France as were the study of classical authors and many other forms of intellectual activity.[63] After the beginning of the fourteenth century, this Italian Aristotelianism assumed a more definite shape.[64] The teaching of logic and natural philosophy became a well established part of the university curriculum and even spread to some of the secondary schools. An increasing number of commentaries and questions on the works of Aristotle reflect this teaching tradition, and numerous systematic treatises on philosophical subjects show the same general trend and background. During the fourteenth and fifteenth centuries, further influences were received from Paris in the field of natural philosophy and from Oxford in the field of logic;[65] and from the latter part of the fourteenth century on we can trace an unbroken tradition of Italian Aristotelianism which continued through the fifteenth and sixteenth century and far into the seventeenth century.[66]

The common notion that scholasticism as an old philosophy was superseded by the new philosophy of humanism is thus again disproved by plain facts. For Italian scholasticism originated toward the end of the thirteenth century, that is, about the same time as did Italian humanism, and both traditions developed side by side throughout the period of the Renaissance and even thereafter.

However, the two traditions had their locus and center in two different sectors of learning: humanism in the field of grammar, rhetoric, and poetry and to some extent in moral philosophy, scholasticism in the fields of logic and of natural philosophy. Everybody knows the eloquent attacks launched by Petrarch and Bruni against the logicians of their time, and it is generally believed that these attacks represent a vigorous new movement rebelling against an old entrenched habit of thought. Yet actually the English method of dialectic was quite as novel at the Italian schools of that time as were the humanistic studies advocated by Petrarch and Bruni,[67] and the humanistic attack was as much a matter of departmental rivalry as it was a clash of opposite ideas or philosophies. Bruni is even hinting at one point that he is not speaking quite in earnest.[68] Such controversies, interesting as they are, were mere episodes in a long period of peaceful coexistence between humanism and scholasticism. Actually the humanists quarreled as much among each other as they did with the scholastics. Moreover, it would be quite wrong to consider these controversies as serious battles for basic principles whereas many of them were meant to be merely personal feuds, intellectual tournaments, or rhetorical exercises. Finally, any attempt to reduce these controversies to one issue must fail since the discussions were concerned with many diverse and overlapping issues.[69] Therefore, we should no longer be surprised that Italian Aristotelianism quietly and forcefully survived the attacks of Petrarch and his humanist successors.

But the Aristotelianism of the Renaissance did not remain untouched by the new influence of humanism. Philosophers began to make abundant use of the Greek text and of the new Latin translations of Aristotle, of his ancient commentators, and of other Greek thinkers. The revival of ancient philosophies that came in the wake of the humanistic movement, especially the revival of Platonism and of Stoicism, left a strong impact upon the Aristotelian philosophers of the Renaissance.[70] Yet in spite of these significant modifications, Renaissance Aristotelianism continued the medieval scholastic tradition without any visible break. It preserved a firm hold on the university chairs of logic, natural philosophy, and metaphysics, whereas even the humanist professors of moral philosophy continued to base their lectures on Aristotle. The literary activity of these Aristotelian philosophers is embodied in a large number of commentaries, questions, and treatises. This literature is difficult of access and arduous to read, but rich in philosophical problems and doctrines. It represents the bulk and kernel of the philosophical thought of the period, but it has been badly neglected by modern historians. Scholars hostile to the Middle Ages considered this literature an unfortunate survival of medieval traditions that may be safely disregarded, whereas the true modern spirit of the Renaissance is expressed in the literature of the humanists. Medievalists, on the other hand, have largely concentrated on the earlier phases of scholastic philosophy and gladly sacrificed the later scholastics to the criticism of the humanists and their modern followers, a tendency that has been further accentuated by the recent habit of identifying scholasticism with Thomism.

Consequently, most modern scholars have condemned the Aristotelian philosophers of the Renaissance without a hearing, labeling them as empty squibblers and as followers of a dead past who failed to understand the living problems of their new times. Recent works on the civilization of the Renaissance thus often repeat the charges made against the Aristotelian philosophers by the humanists of their time, and even give those attacks a much more extreme meaning than they were originally intended to have. Other scholars who are not favorable to the humanists either include both scholastics and humanists in a summary sentence that reflects the judgments of seventeenth-century scientists and philosophers. Only a few famous figures such as Pietro Pomponazzi seem to resist the general verdict.

There has been a tendency to present Pomponazzi and a few other thinkers as basically different from the other Aristotelians of their time and as closely related with the humanists or with the later scientists. This is merely an attempt to reconcile the respect for Pomponazzi with modern preconceptions against the Aristotelians of the Renaissance. Actually Pomponazzi does not belong to the humanists or to the later scientists, but to the tradition of medieval and Renaissance Aristotelianism. The number of modern scholars who have actually read some of the works of the Italian Aristotelians is comparatively small. The most influential comprehensive treatment of the group is found in Renan's book on Averroes and Averroism, a book which had considerable merits for its time, but which also contains several errors and confusions which have been repeated ever since.[71] If we want to judge the merits and limitations of

Renaissance Aristotelianism we will have to proceed to a new direct investigation of the source materials, instead of repeating antiquated judgments. It will be necessary to study in detail the questions discussed by these thinkers, such as the doctrine of immortality and its demonstrability, the problem of the so-called double truth, and the method of scientific proof.[72] Due consideration should also be given to the contributions made by these Aristotelian philosophers to medicine and natural history, and to the influence they exercised upon such early scientists as Galilei and Harvey.[73] Current notions about the prevalence of Thomism among the Aristotelians, about the controversy of the Averroists and the Alexandrists, about the continuity and uniformity of the school of Padua, and even the very concept of Averroism will have to be reexamined and possibly abandoned. Also the widespread belief that the Italian Aristotelians were atheists and free-thinkers who merely did not dare to say what they thought must be investigated in its origin and validity.[74]

Thus we may conclude that the humanism and the scholasticism of the Renaissance arose in medieval Italy about the same time, that is, about the end of the thirteenth century, and that they coexisted and developed all the way through and beyond the Renaissance period as different branches of learning. Their controversy, much less persistent and violent than usually represented, is merely a phase in the battle of the arts, not a struggle for existence. We may compare it to the debates of the arts in medieval literature, to the rivaling claims of medicine and of law at the universities, or to the claims advanced by Leonardo in his *Paragone* for the superiority of painting over the other arts. Humanism certainly had a tendency to influence the other sciences and to expand at their expense, but all kinds of adjustments and combinations between humanism and scholasticism were possible and were successfully accomplished.

It is only after the Renaissance, through the rise of modern science and modern philosophy, that Aristotelianism was gradually displaced, whereas humanism became gradually detached from its rhetorical background and evolved into modern philology and history.

Thus humanism and scholasticism both occupy an important place in the civilization of the Italian Renaissance, yet neither represents a unified picture, nor do both together constitute the whole of Renaissance civilization. Just as humanism and scholasticism coexisted as different branches of culture, there were besides them other important, and perhaps even more important branches. I am thinking of the developments in the fine arts, in vernacular literature, in the mathematical sciences, and in religion and theology. Many misunderstandings have resulted from the attempts to interpret or to criticize humanism and scholasticism in the light of these other developments. Too many historians have tried to play up the fine arts, or vernacular poetry, or science, or religion against the "learning of the schools." These attempts must be rejected. The religious and theological problems of the Protestant and Catholic Reformation were hardly related to the issues discussed in the philosophical literature of the same time, and supporters and enemies of humanistic learning and of Aristotelian philosophy were found among the followers of both religious parties. The development of vernacular poetry in Italy was not opposed or delayed by the humanists, as most historians of literature complain. Some humanists stressed the superiority of Latin, to be sure, but few if any of them seriously thought of abolishing the *volgare* in speech or writing. On the other hand, many humanists are found among the advocates of the *volgare,* and a great number of authors continued to write in both languages. Again, modern historians have tried to interpret as a struggle for existence what in fact was merely a rivalry between different forms of expression.[75]

The admirable development of the fine arts which is the chief glory of the Italian Renaissance did not spring from any exaggerated notions about the creative genius of the artist or about his role in society and culture. Such notions are the product of the Romantic movement and its eighteenth-century forerunners, and they were largely foreign to the Italian Renaissance.[75a] Renaissance artists were primarily craftsmen, and they often became scientists, not because their superior genius anticipated the modern destinies of science, but because certain branches of scientific knowledge, such as anatomy, perspective, or mechanics were considered as a necessary requirement in the development of their craft. If some of these artist-scientists were able to make considerable contributions to science, this does not mean that they were completely independent or contemptuous of the science and learning available in their time.

Finally, mathematics and astronomy made remarkable progress during the sixteenth century and assumed increasing importance in their practical applications, in the literature of the time, and in the curriculum of the schools and universities. If this development did not immediately affect philosophy, this was due not to the stupidity or inertia of contemporary philosophers, but to the fact that physics or natural philosophy was considered as a part of philosophy and that there was almost no traditional link between the mathematical sciences and philosophy. Galileo was a professional student and teacher of mathematics and astronomy, not of philosophy. His claim that physics should be based on mathematics rather than on logic was not merely a novel idea as far as it went, but it revolutionized the very conceptions on which the curriculum of the schools and universities was based. It is hence quite understandable that he was opposed by the Aristotelian physicists of his time who considered his method as an invasion of their traditional domain by the mathematicians. On the other hand, there is no evidence that Galileo met with any serious resistance within his own field of mathematics and astronomy in which the main chairs were soon occupied by his pupils. If we want to understand and to judge these developments we must know the issues and the professional traditions of the later Middle Ages and of the Renaissance.

Modern scholarship has been far too much influenced by all kinds of prejudices, against the use of Latin, against scholasticism, against the medieval church, and also by the unwarranted effort to read later developments, such as the German Reformation, or French libertinism, or nineteenth-century liberalism or nationalism, back into the Renaissance. The only way to understand the Renaissance is a direct and, possibly, an objective study of the original sources. We have no real justification to take sides in the controversies of the Renaissance, and to play up humanism against scholasticism, or scholasticism against humanism, or modern science against both of them. Instead of trying to reduce everything to one or two issues, which is the privilege and curse of political controversy, we should try to develop a kind of historical pluralism. It is easy to praise everything in the past which happens to resemble certain favorite ideas of our own time, or to ridicule and minimize everything that disagrees with them. This method is neither fair nor helpful for an adequate understanding of the past. It is equally easy to indulge in a sort of worship of success, and to dismiss defeated and refuted ideas with a shrugging of the shoulders, but just as in political history, this method does justice neither to the vanquished nor to the victors. Instead of blaming each century for not having anticipated the achievements of the next, intellectual history must patiently register the errors of the past as well as its truths. Complete objectivity may be impossible to achieve, but it should remain the permanent aim and standard of the historian as well as of the philosopher and scientist.

6. THE PHILOSOPHY OF MAN IN THE ITALIAN RENAISSANCE

THE achievements of the Italian Renaissance in the fine arts, in poetry and literature, in historiography and political thought, and in the natural sciences are well known, and they have been explored and emphasized in a number of valuable recent studies. The contributions of Renaissance Italy to learning and to philosophy are perhaps less widely understood, if I am not mistaken. To be sure, the group of natural philosophers of the later sixteenth century, which culminated in Giordano Bruno, has attracted some attention, mainly for their influence on the rise of early science. Yet I shall concentrate on the earlier phases of Renaissance thought, which have been the center of my studies for a number of years, and accordingly, I shall emphasize, not the philosophy of nature, but the philosophy of man. I shall briefly discuss the three major currents which dominated the development of Italian thought between 1350 and 1520: Humanism, Platonism, and Aristotelianism.

In our contemporary discussion, the term "Humanism" has become one of those slogans which through their very vagueness carry an almost universal and irresistible appeal. Every person interested in "human values" or in "human welfare" is nowadays called a "humanist," and there is hardly any person who would not like to be, or pretend to be, a humanist in this sense of the word. I am afraid that, for the purposes of this essay, we shall have to revise the modern-day definition of the term "humanism." For the humanism of the Renaissance was something quite different from that of the present day. To be sure, Renaissance humanists were also interested in human values, but this was incidental to their major concern, which was the study and imitation of classical, Greek and Latin literature. This classical human-ism of the Italian Renaissance was primarily a cultural, liter-ary, and educational movement, and although it had a definite impact upon Renaissance thought, its philosophical ideas can never be completely detached from its literary interests. The term "humanism" as applied to the classicist movement of the Renaissance was coined by historians of the nineteenth century, but the terms "humanities" and "humanist" were coined during the Renaissance itself. Already some ancient Roman authors used the term *Studia humanitatis* to ennoble the study of poetry, literature, and history, and this expres-sion was taken up by the scholars of the early Italian Renais-sance to stress the human value of the fields of study which they cultivated: grammar, rhetoric, poetry, history, and moral philosophy, in the sense in which these fields were understood at that time. Soon the professional teacher of these subjects came to be called *humanista,* a "humanist," a term which occurred first in documents of the late fifteenth century and became increasingly common during the sixteenth century.

The origin of Italian humanism is usually attributed to Petrarch who had a few forerunners, to be sure, but accord-ing to the common view, no real predecessors. There is no doubt that Petrarch was the first really great figure among the Italian humanists. Yet some of the characteristic inter-ests and tendencies of Italian humanism preceded Petrarch at least by one generation. The origin and rise of Italian humanism, in my opinion, was due to two, or rather three, different factors. One factor was the native Italian tradition of medieval rhetoric, which had been cultivated by teachers and notaries, and handed down as a technique of composing letters, documents, and speeches. The second factor was the so-called medieval humanism, that is, the study of classi-cal Latin poetry and literature, which had flourished in the schools of the twelfth century, especially in France, and to which Italy at that time had made a very limited contribution. Toward the end of the thirteenth century, this study of the Latin classics was introduced into the Italian schools and merged with the native rhetorical tradition that had been of a much more practical nature. Thus the scholarly study of the Latin classics began to develop, once the successful imitation of the classical authors, based on their careful study, was considered as the best training for those who wanted to write and to speak well, in prose and in verse, in Latin and in the vernacular. A third factor was added to this development during the latter half of the fourteenth century: the study of classical Greek literature, which had been almost unknown to the Western Middle Ages, but had been cultivated through the centuries in the Byzantine Empire and was now brought to Italy from the East as a result of intensified political, ecclesiastic, and scholarly contacts.

The fruit of this combination of scholarly interests was the body of humanistic learning which comprised Latin and Greek grammar, eloquence, poetry, history, and moral philosophy. The humanists occupied the chairs of all these fields at the universities, asserted their importance in relation to the other sciences, and obtained almost complete control of the secondary schools in which grammar and rhetoric always had been the core of the curriculum.

The humanists also acquired considerable prestige and power through the places they held in the various professions. For the humanists were not merely free-lance writers, as it is often asserted, and the case of Petrarch is by no means typical. Most of the humanists belonged to one of three professional groups, and sometimes to more than one at the same time: they were teachers at the universities or secondary schools; or they were secretaries of princes or cities; or they were noble or wealthy amateurs who combined their business or political activities with the fashionable intellectual interests of their time. This professional and social place of the humanists easily explains the range and content of their literary production. They edited, translated, and expounded classical Greek and Latin authors, and wrote on matters of grammar and philology; they composed speeches, letters, poems, historical works, and moral treatises. The bulk of this humanistic literature is enormous, and on the whole it is much more interesting than those who have never read it would have us believe. Much, although not all, of this literature is written in Latin, which accounts in part for the scanty interest it has encountered in recent years. The charge that the works of the humanists are studded with classical quotations and with rhetorical phrases is to some extent correct. Yet we must add that the humanists managed to express in this classicist and rhetorical Latin the nuances of their own personal experience and the realities of contemporary life. A Neo-latin literature which contains descriptions of tournaments, and of snowball fights in the streets of fifteenth-century Florence certainly cannot be dismissed as academic, although its means of expression may be less accessible to us than are the paintings of the same period that reflect similar standards of form and content.

Within the framework of Renaissance learning, humanism certainly occupied a very important place. However, it would be quite wrong to assume, as modern scholars often do, that humanism represents the complete picture of Renaissance science and philosophy, and that it tended, or even hoped, to expel and to replace all those traditions of medieval learning that are usually associated with the term "scholasticism." Humanism originated and developed within the limited area of rhetorical and philological studies. In asserting the claims of their own field, the humanists were apt to become aggressive toward their colleagues in other disciplines, but they were quite unable to provide for those other fields a subject matter capable of replacing the material furnished by the medieval tradition. Humanism was and remained a cultural and literary movement bound by its classical and rhetorical interests. Its influence on other fields, such as natural philosophy, theology, law, medicine, or mathematics, could be only external and indirect.

However, this indirect influence was in many respects quite important, especially in the case of philosophical thought with which we are primarily concerned. The humanistic movement of the Renaissance provided philosophers with new standards of literary elegance and of historical criticism, with additional classical source materials, and consequently with many ancient ideas and philosophies which thus came to be restated and revived or to be combined with other old and new doctrines. Moreover, although humanism in itself was not committed to any particular philosophy, it contained in its very program a few general ideas that were of great importance for Renaissance thought. One of these ideas was the conception the humanists had of history and of their own historical position. They believed that classical antiquity was in most respects a perfect age; that it was followed by a long period of decline, the Dark or Middle Ages; and that it was the task and destiny of their own age to accomplish a rebirth or renaissance of classical antiquity, or of its learning, arts, and sciences. The humanists themselves thus helped to shape the concept of the Renaissance which has been so bitterly criticized by certain modern historians.

Even more important was the emphasis on man which was inherent in the cultural and educational program of the Renaissance humanists and which should endear them even to our contemporary "humanists" (although the latter would show slight sympathy for the educational ideals of their Renaissance predecessors). When the Renaissance humanists called their studies the "humanities" or *Studia humanitatis,* they expressed the claim that these studies contribute to the education of a desirable human being, and hence are of vital concern for man as man. Thus they indicated a basic concern for man and his dignity, and this aspiration became quite explicit in many of their writings. When Petrarch whom we called the first great humanist describes in a famous letter his trip to the peak of Mont Ventoux, he tells us that overwhelmed by the marvelous view, he took Augustine's *Confessions* out of his pocket and opened it at random. He found the following passage: "Men go to admire the heights of mountains, the great floods of the sea, the courses of rivers, the shores of the ocean, and the orbits of the stars, and neglect themselves." "I was stunned," Petrarch continues, "closed the book and was angry at myself since I was still admiring earthly things although I should have learned long ago from pagan philosophers that nothing is admirable but the soul in comparison to which, if it is great, nothing is great."[1] Petrarch thus expresses his conviction that man and his soul are the true standard of intellectual importance, but in doing so, he uses the very words of Augustine, the Christian classic, and of Seneca, the pagan classic.

About the middle of the fifteenth century, the Florentine humanist, Giannozzo Manetti, composed a lengthy treatise on the dignity and excellence of man, which was written as a conscious reply to Pope Innocent III's treatise on the miserable condition of mankind. Manetti's work is filled with quotations from Cicero and from Lactantius.[2] Also among later humanists, the dignity of man continued to be a favorite topic. None of them expressed the link between this concern for man and the admiration of antiquity more clearly than the great author who has been called a vernacular humanist.[3] For Machiavelli who in his enforced retirement liked to put on evening clothes to converse with the great ancient writers, the study of the ancients was valuable because they were human models, and the attempt to imitate them was not vain since human nature is always the same.[4]

Whereas the humanistic movement had a literary and

cultural origin and character and hence had merely an indirect, though powerful, influence on the development of philosophical thought, the second great intellectual movement of the early Renaissance, Platonism, was philosophical in its origin and had but an incidental, though very significant, impact upon Renaissance literature. Considering the quantity of its literary production and the number of its followers, Platonism was not as broad a current as was humanism, but it was much deeper, both in the wealth of its ideas and in the response it evoked from its adherents. Platonism, to be sure, had its own centers in such informal and temporary circles as the Platonic Academy of Florence, as well as in certain literary Academies of the sixteenth century and in a few university chairs of Platonic philosophy. Yet taken as a whole, Platonism did not possess the strong institutional and professional support which both humanism and Aristotelianism were enjoying. Platonism owed its influence rather to the personal appeal of its ideas to the experiences and inclinations of individual thinkers and writers, an appeal that varied in depth and sincerity and that sometimes, as things go, degenerated into a mere fashion.

The Platonism of the Italian Renaissance as it culminated in Marsilio Ficino, the leader of the Florentine Academy, and in his friend and pupil, Giovanni Pico della Mirandola, was in many respects an offshoot of the humanistic movement. Both Ficino and Pico had enjoyed a thorough humanistic education and were imbued with the stylistic and classicist standards of the humanists. Their preference for Plato had its antecedents in Petrarch and in other early humanists. Ficino's endeavor to translate and to expound the works of Plato and of the ancient Neoplatonists was comparable to the work done by the humanists on other classical authors. His attempt to restate and to revive the teachings of Platonism reflected the general trend toward reviving ancient arts, ideas, and institutions and in one of his

letters, he compared his own revival of Platonic philosophy
to the rebirth of grammar, poetry, rhetoric, painting, sculp-
ture, architecture, music, and astronomy which had been accomplished in his century.[5] However Renaissance Platonism
had other roots outside the traditions and interests of early
humanism. One of these roots was the Aristotelianism or
scholasticism of the later Middle Ages which continued to
dominate the teaching of philosophy at the universities and
other schools. We know beyond any doubt that Ficino absorbed this kind of training as a student at the University
of Florence, whereas it had never been questioned that Pico
had studied scholastic philosophy at the universities of Padua
and of Paris. This training left profound traces in their
thought and writings. It enabled them to proceed beyond
the amateurish and vague ideas of the earlier humanists to
a serious and methodical kind of philosophical speculation
which could have an influence on professionally trained
philosophers and which was taken seriously even by their
philosophical opponents. Consequently, Ficino and Pico
abandoned the superficial polemic of the earlier humanists
against scholastic philosophy, and gladly acknowledged their
indebtedness to Aristotle and to the medieval thinkers. In
an interesting correspondence with Ermolao Barbaro, Pico
took up the defense of the medieval philosophers, stressing
the point that philosophical content is much more important
than literary form.[6] Another source of Renaissance Platonism, which distinguishes it both from humanism and
Aristotelianism, was the heritage of medieval mysticism and
Augustinianism. Even after the thirteenth century when
Aristotelianism had become predominant in the teaching of
philosophy and theology, the older current of Augustinianism survived among the Franciscan theologians, and in a
vaguer form in the growing popular religious literature
which developed around the religious associations for laymen. There are several indications that Ficino was strongly

influenced by this brand of religious spiritualism, and Pico's later writings and his relationship to Savonarola show that he had similar inclinations. If we realize that Ficino's Academy resembled in many respects such an association of laymen in which classical scholarship and secular philosophy were added to a basically religious atmosphere, we can better understand the impression which this Academy made upon the educated circles of Medicean Florence, and upon the imagination of later generations.[6a]

Due to these additional philosophical and religious resources, Platonism was able to transform some of the vague ideas and aspirations of the early humanists into definite and elaborate speculative theories. Especially did the emphasis on man which had been one of the most characteristic aspirations of early humanist thought receive a more systematic philosophical expression in the works of the Renaissance Platonists.

Ficino's major philosophical work, the *Platonic Theology,* contains several passages in which the excellence and dignity of man is emphasized. Man is superior to other creatures in the variety of his arts and skills. With his thought and with his desire, he passes through all parts of the universe, is related to all of them, and has a share in them all. The human soul is directed both toward God and toward the body, that is, both toward the intelligible and toward the corporeal world. Hence it participates both in time and in eternity. These ideas are embodied in Ficino's scheme of a universal hierarchy in which the human soul occupies a privileged, central place: God, the Angelic Mind, the Rational Soul, Quality, and Body. Due to its central position, the soul is able to mediate between the upper and the lower half of reality, between the intelligible and the corporeal. Ficino who had borrowed many elements of his scheme from Neoplatonic tradition, consciously modified it in this decisive point, the central position of the human soul.

"This (the soul) is the greatest of all miracles in nature. All other things beneath God are always one single being, but the soul is all things together . . . Therefore it may be rightly called the center of nature, the middle term of all things, the series of the world, the face of all, the bond and juncture of the universe."[7]

The same idea is taken up and further developed by Pico in his famous *Oration* on the dignity of man. Pico stresses especially man's freedom to choose his way of life. Consequently, man no longer occupies any fixed place in the universal hierarchy, not even the privileged central place, but he is entirely detached from that hierarchy and constitutes a world in himself. Illustrating this conception with a story, Pico recounts that man was created last among all things when God had already distributed all His gifts among the other creatures. "Finally, the Best of Workmen decided that that to which nothing of its very own could be given should be given, in composite fashion, whatsoever had belonged individually to each and everything . . . and He spoke to him as follows: We have given thee, Adam, no fixed seat, no form of thy very own, no gift peculiarly thine, that . . . thou mayest . . . possess as thine own the seat, the form, the gifts which thou thyself shalt desire . . . In conformity with thy free judgment in whose hands I have placed thee, thou art confined by no bonds, and thou wilt fix the limits of thy nature for thyself . . . Neither heavenly nor earthly, neither mortal nor immortal have We made thee. Thou . . . art the moulder and maker of thyself . . . Thou canst grow downward into the lower natures which are brutes. Thou canst again grow upward from the mind's reason into the higher natures which are divine."[8]

The concern for man and the meaning of his life determines also another basic theory of Ficino, the doctrine of immortality to which he devotes the largest part of his chief philosophical work, the *Platonic Theology*. Ficino does not condemn or minimize the practical activities of life, but he states with great emphasis that the main purpose of human life is contemplation. By contemplation he understands a spiritual experience which begins with a detachment of our mind from the outside world, which then proceeds through various degrees of knowledge and desire, and finally culminates in the immediate vision and enjoyment of God. Since this final union with God is rarely attained during the present life, Ficino postulates a future life in which this aim will be attained in a permanent fashion by all those who made the necessary effort during the present life. The immortality of the soul thus becomes the center of Ficino's philosophy, because immortality is needed to justify his interpretation of human existence as a continuing effort of contemplation. Without immortality, that effort would be vain, and human existence would be without any attainable end. On the other hand, a philosophy which thus centers around the theory of immortality is primarily concerned with man and his purpose, both in the present and in the future life. This concern for man and the immortality of his soul explains certain statements of Ficino which have shocked some modern theologians. For he says that "man worships the eternal God for the sake of the future life,"[9] and once he exclaims: "How does it help you, O theologian, to attribute eternity to God, if you do not attribute it to yourself in order that you may enjoy divine eternity through your own eternity?"[10] Ficino also links the doctrine of immortality with the dignity of man when he argues that man, the most perfect of all animals, would be more miserable than the beasts if, through the lack of immortality, he alone were deprived of attaining the natural end of his existence.[11]

The central place in the universe, and the immortality of the soul are privileges in which potentially every human being has a share, yet their actual significance depends on the individual and solitary effort of each person, and on his share in the contemplative life. However, in his theory of love and friendship, Ficino also gives a philosophical significance to the relationship between several persons. He does not condemn or disregard sexual love, to be sure, yet in his famous theory of Platonic love and friendship he is merely concerned with that spiritual relationship which is established between two or more persons through the share which each of them individually has in the contemplative life. In a true friendship, he claims, there are always at least three partners, two human beings, and God who founds their friendship.[12] In this way, Ficino established a direct link between the highest form of human relationship and the most intimate and personal experience of contemplative life. Hence he could proclaim that friendship understood in this sense was the spiritual tie that linked the members of his Platonic Academy with each other and with himself, their common master. This theory of Platonic love and friendship had a tremendous appeal to Ficino's contemporaries and to the successive generations of the sixteenth century who wrote about it again and again in prose and in verse. The term "Platonic love" has since acquired a somewhat curious connotation, and it certainly would be difficult to defend all the vagaries contained in the love treatises of the later Renaissance. However, it is important to realize that the doctrine in its origin had a serious philosophical meaning, and that it was taken up so eagerly because it provided educated persons with a more or less superficial spiritual interpretation for their personal feelings and passions. The rather complex background of the theory which had its roots in ancient theories of love and friendship, in Christian traditions of charity and spiritual fellowship, and in medieval conceptions of courtly love, could only increase its popularity in a period in which all those currents were still very much alive.

For the Florentine Platonists, the concept of man and

his dignity was not merely limited to the solitary experiences
and to the personal relationships of individuals, but it also
led to the conscious awareness of a solidarity of all men
which imposed definite moral and intellectual obligations
upon each individual. This attitude is implied in Ficino's
views about religion and its various kinds. He emphasizes
that Christianity is the most perfect religion, to be sure, but
he also asserts that religion as such is natural to all men and
distinguishes them from the animals. The variety of reli-
gions contributes to the beauty of the universe, and each
religion, at least in an indirect and unconscious manner, is
related to the one, true God. Pico goes even further and
emphasizes that all religious and philosophical traditions
have a share in a common, universal truth. Pagan, Jewish,
and Christian theologians, and also all philosophers who
supposedly contradict each other, Plato and Aristotle, Avicenna and Averroes, Thomas and Scotus, and many others
have had a good many insights into truth. When Pico
included propositions from all these authors among his nine
hundred theses, it was his underlying intention to illustrate
this universality of truth which justified his endeavor to incorporate and defend doctrines from so many different
sources. This syncretism of Pico which has been rightly
emphasized in a recent study,[13] really provided the foundation for a broad conception of religious and philosophical
tolerance.

In a different manner, the solidarity of mankind is expressed in Ficino's conception of *humanitas*. The Latin
term is ambiguous since it stands both for the human race,
and for humane feeling as a personal virtue. This ambiguity reflects the ancient Roman Stoic ideal of *humanitas*
that combined with the standards of cultural refinement a
high respect for other persons as fellow human beings.[13a]
This concept was taken up and further elaborated by Ficino.
Starting from the general notion that love and attraction

constitute a force of unification in all parts of the universe, he applies it in particular to mankind as a natural species. Man proves himself a member of the human race by loving other men as his equals, by being humane. When he is inhumane and cruel, he removes himself from the community of mankind and forfeits his human dignity. "Why are boys crueler than old men?" Ficino asks in a letter to Tommaso Minerbetti. "Insane men crueler than intelligent men? Dull men crueler than the ingenious? Because they are, as it were, less men than the others. Therefore the cruel men are called inhumane and brutal. In general those who are far removed from the perfect nature of man by fault of age, a vice of the soul, a sickness of the body, or by an inimical position of the stars, hate and neglect the human species as something foreign and alien. Nero was, so to speak, not a man, but a monster, being akin to man only by his skin. Had he really been a man, he would have loved other men as members of the same body. For as individual men are under one Idea and in one species, they are like one man. Therefore, I believe, the sages called by the name of man himself only that one among all the virtues that loves and helps all men as brothers deriving in a long series from one father, in other words, humanity."[14]

Even Ficino's theory of immortality is influenced by this sense of human solidarity. Ficino admits that the immediate vision of God can be attained in earthly life by a few individuals, but this is not considered as a sufficient fulfillment of the natural desire inherent in all men. The postulate of a future life must be maintained in order that this desire be fulfilled, if not for all men, at least for all those who tried to direct their efforts toward God. Ficino does not teach with Origen that there will be a final salvation of all souls, but he leaves us with the impression that a reasonable proportion of mankind will attain eternal happiness, the true goal of earthly existence and of human life.

The third intellectual current of the early Renaissance, Aristotelianism, had its roots in the teaching traditions of the later Middle Ages. At the Italian Universities, the study of Aristotelian philosophy obtained a permanent place about the end of the thirteenth century. From its very beginning, this study was linked with medicine, not with theology. Consequently, it centered around natural philosophy, and to a lesser extent around logic. The so-called theory of double truth which characterizes the tendency of this school was meant to recognize the authority of the Church in the domain of dogmatic theology, and at the same time to preserve the independence of philosophical thought within the limits of natural reason. These Aristotelian philosophers disagreed among each other on many issues and were divided into several opposing schools, yet they had common problems, common source materials, and a common method. In contrast to the humanists and to the Platonists, the Aristotelians represent the solid, professional tradition of philosophy. They dominated the teaching of philosophy down to the end of the Renaissance, and their numerous commentaries and treatises reflect the methods and interests of that teaching. Their share in the intellectual life of the Renaissance was much larger than most scholars seem to realize, and they were by no means as foreign to the new problems of their own times as often asserted. Renaissance Aristotelianism developed without a break from the traditions of medieval Aristotelianism, to be sure, but it also assimilated many significant elements from the humanism and Platonism of its own time.

It is easy to illustrate this with the example of the most famous Aristotelian philosopher of the Italian Renaissance, Pietro Pomponazzi. He had received his training at Padua, and spent his later and most productive years as a professor of philosophy at Bologna. Pomponazzi was thoroughly familiar with the ideas and writings of his medieval predecessors and discussed in part the same problems, with the same method of reasoning, and on the basis of the same texts of Aristotle. Yet he was indebted to the humanists for his knowledge of the Greek commentators of Aristotle, and of non-Aristotelian ancient thought, especially of Stoicism. He also utilized the writings of the Platonists and discussed or appropriated some of their ideas. This affinity of Pomponazzi with the humanists and Platonists of his time is especially apparent in his conception of man.

Pomponazzi's concern for man is already expressed in the fact that, like Ficino, he dedicated one of his most important philosophical works to the problem of immortality. As a result of its highly provocative position, this treatise became the starting point of a lively controversy among Aristotelian philosophers and theologians which continued for many decades. In approaching the problem of immortality, Pomponazzi emphasizes with the Platonists that man occupies a middle place in the universe. "I held that the beginning of our consideration should be this: that man is not of simple but of multiple, not of fixed, but of an ambiguous, nature, and is placed in the middle between mortal and immortal things . . . Hence the ancients rightly placed him between eternal and temporal things, since he is neither purely eternal nor purely temporal, because he participates in both natures. And existing thus in the middle, he has the power to assume either nature."[15]

Yet in spite of this starting point, Pomponazzi proceeds to an analysis that in many respects is the exact opposite of Ficino's. The human intellect is not material in its substance, to be sure, but its knowledge is entirely limited to corporeal objects. This is the manner in which it occupies a middle place between the pure intelligences of angels and the souls of animals. There is no evidence whatsoever that man in this life can attain a pure knowledge of intelligible objects. Consequently, there is no rational proof for the immortality of the soul, although immortality must be accepted as an article of faith.

Pomponazzi thus demolishes the ideal of contemplation which finds its necessary fulfillment in a future life. He substitutes for it the ideal of a moral virtue which can be attained during the present life. Thus the dignity of man is not only maintained, but man's present, earthly life is credited with a significance that does not depend on any hopes or fears for the future. Pomponazzi states this view in simple sentences that remind us of Plato and the ancient Stoics as well as of Spinoza and Kant. "There are two kinds of reward and punishment: one is essential and inseparable, the other accidental and separable. The essential reward of virtue is virtue itself which makes man happy. For human nature cannot attain anything higher than virtue. It alone makes man secure and removed from all trouble . . . The opposite applies to vice. The punishment of the vicious person is vice itself which is more miserable and unhappy than anything else . . . Accidental reward is more imperfect than essential reward, for gold is more imperfect than virtue; and accidental punishment is less heavy than essential punishment. For a penalty is an accidental punishment, whereas guilt is an essential punishment. Yet the punishment of guilt is much worse than that of a penalty. Therefore, it does not matter if sometimes the accidental is omitted provided that the essential remains. Moreover, when a good receives an accidental reward its essential good seems to decrease and does not remain in its perfection. For example, if someone does a good deed without a hope of reward, and another with a hope of reward, the action of the latter is not considered as good as that of the former. Hence he who receives no accidental reward is more essentially rewarded than he who does. In the same way, he who acts wickedly and receives accidental punishment seems to be less punished than he who receives no accidental punishment. For the punishment of guilt is greater and worse than that of a penalty. And when a penalty is added to guilt, the

latter decreases. Hence he who receives no accidental punishment is more essentially punished than he who does."[16]

The emphasis on moral virtue as the self-contained end
of human life sets, in the first place, a standard of individual
conduct. Yet Pomponazzi, like Ficino, arrives quite consistently at the notion that there is a solidarity of mankind,
and that each individual, through his right actions, makes
his contribution to the universal good. "We must assume
and firmly keep in mind that the entire human race may be
compared to one individual man."[17] All individuals contribute to the good of mankind, just as all members of our
body contribute to the welfare of the entire body. "The
whole human race is like one body composed of various
members which have different functions, but which are suited
for the common usefulness of mankind."[18]

Hence the end of man must be determined in such a way
that it can be attained by all men or at least by many individuals. This consideration prompted Ficino to postulate a
future life in which many individuals will reach the vision of
God which in the present life is experienced only by a few
rare persons. The same consideration leads Pomponazzi
to assert that the primary aim of human life must be found
in moral action, and not in contemplation. This statement
is the more interesting since it is at variance with the teaching of Aristotle. All men, Pomponazzi argues, share to
some extent in three intellectual faculties, that is, in the speculative, the moral, and the technical intellect. Yet the part
which men have in these intellectual faculties is different for
each of them. The speculative intellect is not characteristic
of man as man, but belongs properly to the gods, as Aristotle
says. Although all men have something of it, only very few
possess it, or can possess it, fully and perfectly. On the
other hand, the technical intellect is not characteristic of
man since it is also shared by many animals. "Yet the practical intellect truly belongs to man. For every normal hu-

man being can attain it perfectly, and according to it a person is called good or bad in an absolute sense, whereas according to the speculative or technical intellect, a person is called good or bad only in some respect and with qualifications. For a man is called a good man or a bad man with regard to his virtues and vices. Yet a good metaphysician is not called a good man, but a good metaphysician, and a good architect is not called good in an absolute sense, but a good architect. Therefore, a man is not angry when he is not called a metaphysician, a philosopher, or a carpenter. Yet he is most angry when he is said to be a thief, intemperate, unjust, foolish, or something wicked of that sort, as if to be good or bad were human and in our power, whereas to be a philosopher or an architect is not in our power nor necessary for a man. Hence all human beings can and must be virtuous, but not all must be philosophers, mathematicians, architects, and the like . . . Hence with regard to the practical intellect which is peculiar to man each man must be perfect. For in order that the entire human race be properly preserved each person must be morally virtuous and as much as possible free of vice . . ."[19]

It has been my intention to show that the three major intellectual currents of the early Renaissance were all concerned with the purpose of human life and with the place of man in the universe, and that this concern found its expression not only in definite standards for individual conduct, but also in a strong sense for human relationships and for the solidarity of mankind. The humanistic movement which in its origin was not philosophical provided the general and still vague ideas and aspirations as well as the ancient source materials. The Platonists and Aristotelians who were professional philosophers with speculative interests and training, took up those vague ideas, developed them into definite philosophical doctrines, and assigned them an important place in their elaborate metaphysical systems.

After the first quarter of the sixteenth century, the intellectual currents of the earlier Renaissance continued to exist, but they were increasingly overshadowed, first by the theological controversies growing out of the Reformation, and later by the developments that led to the rise of modern science and of modern philosophy. Yet the early Renaissance left a heritage that remained effective at least down to the end of the eighteenth century: Renaissance humanism remained alive in the educational and literary traditions of Western Europe and in the study of history and philology; Renaissance Platonism handed down the influence of Plato and Plotinus to all those thinkers who attempted to defend some idealistic form of philosophy; and Renaissance Aristotelianism, although partly superseded by experimental physics and science, gave inspiration to many later currents of free-thought. In the last century in which so much of our present thought has its origin those older ideas and traditions were largely forgotten, except by a few scholarly specialists. Modern positivism, encouraged by scientific progress and material success, seemed to have made all other ideas more or less obsolete. Yet the startling events of our own time have shaken our confidence in the sufficiency, if not in the truth, of positivism. We wonder whether its principles are broad enough to explain our experience and to guide our endeavors. We have become more modest about our own achievements, and hence more willing to learn from the past. In the long line of philosophers and writers who constitute the history and tradition of Western thought, a distinctive place belongs to the humanists, Platonists, and Aristotelians of the early Italian Renaissance. Many of their ideas are merely a matter of historical curiosity, but some of them contain a nucleus of permanent truth and might thus become a message and an inspiration to present-day Italy, and to the rest of mankind.

GENERAL BIBLIOGRAPHY

BARON, H. *The Crisis of the Early Italian Renaissance.* 2 vols., Princeton, 1955.

BOLGAR, R. R. *The Classical Heritage and Its Beneficiaries.* Cambridge, 1954 (and Harper Torchbook, forthcoming 1962).

BOUWSMA, W. *The Interpretation of Rennaissance Humanism.* Washington, 1959.

BURCKHARDT, J. *The Civilization of the Renaissance in Italy.* New York: Harper Torchbook edition, 1958.

CASSIRER, E. *Das Erkenntnisproblem.* vol. I. Berlin, 1922.

——— *Individuum und Kosmos in der Philosophie der Renaissance.* Berlin-Leipzig, 1927; Eng. trans., Harper & Brothers, forthcoming 1962.

CASSIRER, E., P. O. KRISTELLER, AND J. H. RANDALL, eds. *The Renaissance Philosophy of Man.* Chicago, 1948.

CHABOD, F. *Machiavelli and the Renaissance.* Cambridge, Mass., 1958.

CURTIUS, E. R. *European Literature and the Latin Middle Ages* (Eng. trans.). New York, 1953.

DE WULF, M. *Histoire de la philosophie médiévale.* 6th ed. 3 vols. Louvain, 1934–1947.

DUHEM, P. *Etudes sur Léonard de Vinci.* 3 vols. Paris 1906–1913.

FERGUSON, W. K. *The Renaissance in Historical Thought.* Boston, 1948.

GARIN, E. *La filosofia.* 2 vols. Milan, 1947.

——— *Der italienische Humanismus.* Bern, 1947.

GENTILE, G. *La filosofia.* Milan, 1904–1915.

GILSON, E. *History of Christian Philosophy in the Middle Ages.* Eng. Trans., New York, 1955.

GRABMANN, M. *Mittelalterliches Geistesleben.* 3 vols. Munich, 1926–1956.

——— *Die Geschichte der scholastischen Methode.* 2 vols. Freiburg, 1909–1911.

HASKIN, CHARLES H. *Studies in Mediaeval Culture.* Oxford, 1929.

——— *Studies in the History of Mediaeval Science.* 2nd ed. Cambridge, Mass., 1927.

HIGHET, G. *The Classical Tradition.* Oxford, 1949 (and Galaxy paperback, 1957).

KRISTELLER, P. O. *Studies in Renaissance Thought and Letters.* Rome, 1956.

KRISTELLER, P. O., AND J. H. RANDALL. "The Study of the Philosophies of the Renaissance," *Journal of the History of Ideas,* II (1941), 449–496.

MANITIUS, M. *Geschichte der lateinischen Literatur des Mittelalters.* 3 vols. Munich, 1911–1931.

MARROU, H.-I. *History of Education in Antiquity.* Eng. trans., New York, 1956.

NARDI, B. *Saggi sull'Aristotelismo Padovano dal secolo XIV al XVI.* Florence, 1958.

OLSCHKI, L. *Geschichte der neusprachlichen wissenschaftlichen Literatur.* 3 vols. Heidelberg, 1919—Halle, 1927.

PARÉ, G., and others. *La Renaissance du XIIe siècle.* Paris-Ottawa, 1933.

RASHDALL, H. *The Universities of Europe in the Middle Ages.* New ed. by F. M. Powicke and A. B. Emden. 3 vols. Oxford, 1936.

RENUCCI, P. *L'Aventure de l'Humanisme Européen au Moyen Age.* Paris, 1953.

SABBADINI, R. *Le scoperte dei codici latini e greci ne' secoli XIV e XV.* 2 vols. Florence, 1905–1914.

SAITTA, G. *Il pensiero italiano nell' umanesimo e nel rinascimento.* 3 vols. Bologna, 1949–1951.

SANDYS, SIR J. E. *A History of Classical Scholarship.* 3 vols. Cambridge, 1908–1921.

SARTON, G. *Introduction to the History of Science.* 3 vols. Baltimore, 1927–1948.

Storia letteraria d'Italia. Milan: Vallardi. Many vols., especially, V. Rossi, *Il Quattrocento,* 1933.

THORNDIKE, L. *A History of Magic and Experimental Science.* 8 vols. New York, 1923–1958.

TIRABOSCHI, G. *Storia della letteratura italiana.* 25 in 14 vols. Venice, 1823.

TOFFANIN, G. *Storia dell'umanesimo.* 3 vols. Bologna, 1950. Vol. II also in English translation (*History of Humanism.* New York, 1954).

UEBERWEG, F. *Grundriss der Geschichte der Philosophie.* vols. I–III. Berlin, 1924–1928.

ULLMAN, B. L. *Studies in the Italian Renaissance.* Rome, 1955.

VOIGT, G. *Die Wiederbelebung des classischen Althertums.* 3rd ed. 2 vols. Berlin, 1893.

WEISS, R. *The Dawn of Humanism in Italy.* London, 1947.

WOODWARD, WILLIAM H. *Studies in Education during the Age of the Renaissance.* Cambridge, 1906.

―――― *Vittorino da Feltre and other Humanist Educators. Cambridge,* 1905.

ZELLER, E. *Outlines of the History of Greek Philosophy.* New York, 1955.

NOTES

1. THE HUMANIST MOVEMENT

1. J. Burckhardt, *The Civilization of the Renaissance in Italy* (New York: Harper Torchbooks, 1958); J. A. Symonds, *Renaissance in Italy,* 7 vols. (London, 1875–1886); J. Huizinga, *The Waning of the Middle Ages* (London, 1924; also Anchor Paperback, 1953); Wallace K. Ferguson, *The Renaissance in Historical Thought* (Boston, 1948); E. Panofsky, "Renaissance and Renascences." *Kenyon Review,* VI (1944), 201–236; discussion on the Renaissance by D. Durand, H. Baron, and others, in *Journal of the History of Ideas,* IV (1943), 1–74; and see below, Ch. 5.

2. *The Battle of the Seven Arts . . . by Hendi d'Andeli,* ed. L. J. Patow (Berkeley, 1914); E. Norden, *Die antike Kunstprosa,* II (Leipzig, 1898), 688ff and 724ff.

3. For some influential definitions of humanism, with which I happen to disagree, see: E. Gilson, *Saint Thomas d'Aquin* (Paris, 1925), 6–7; The same, "Humanisme médiéval et Renaissance," in his *Les Idées et les Lettres* (Paris, 1932), 189ff; Douglas Bush, *The Renaissance and English Humanism* (Toronto, 1939), 39ff; The same, *Classical Influences in Renaissance Literature* (Cambridge, Mass., 1952) 48ff; Gerald G. Walsh, *Medieval Humanism* (New York, 1942), 1: "Humanism, in general, I take to be the idea that a human being is meant to achieve, during life, a fair measure of human happiness" (by that definition, Aristotle is a humanist, but Petrarch is not); Renucci, *L'Aventure de l'Humanisme Européen au Moyen Age* (Paris, 1953), 9.

4. W. Rüegg, *Cicero und der Humanismus* (Zurich, 1946), 1ff.

5. See below, Ch. 5.; A. Campana, "The Origin of the Word 'Humanist,'" *Journal of the Warburg and Courtauld Institutes,* IX (1946), 60–73.

6. W. Jaeger, *Humanism and Theology* (Milwaukee, 1943), 20ff, 72ff; R. Pfeiffer, *Humanitas Erasmiana* (Leipzig-Berlin, 1931).

7. See below, Ch. 5.

8. As has been done, to a certain extent, by E. Garin (*Der italienische Humanismus,* Bern, 1947).

9. H. von Arnim, *Leben und Werke des Dio von Prusa* (Berlin, 1898), 4–114; H. Gomperz, *Sophistik und Rhetorik* (Leipzig, 1912); W. Jaeger, *Paideia,* I (Oxford, 1939, chapter on the Sophists) and III (1944, chapters on Isocrates).

10. R. McKeon, "Rhetoric in the Middle Ages," *Speculum,* XVII (1942), 1–32.

11. A Galletti, *L'Eloquenza* (Milan, 1904–1938).

12. R. Sabbadini, *Le scoperte dei codici latini e greci ne' secoli XIV e XV,* 2 vols. (Florence, 1905–1914). Cf. M. Manitius, *Handschriften antiker Autoren in mittelalterlichen Bibliothekskatalogen* (Leipzig, 1935); G. Billanovich, "Petrarch and the Textual Tradition of Livy," *Journal of the Warburg and Courtauld Institutes,* XIV (1951), 137–208.

13. Louise R. Loomis, *Medieval Hellernism* (Lancaster, Pa. 1906). Valuable recent studies by R. Weiss and others do not fundamentally alter this picture. Yet Sicily and Southern Italy occupy in this respect a place of their own. See: R. Weiss, "The Greek Culture of South Italy in the Later Middle Ages," British Academy, *Proceedings* XXXVII (1951) 23–50; R. Devreesse, *Les Manuscrits grecs de l'Italie Méridionale* (Studi e Testi 183, Vatican City, 1955); Kenneth M. Setton, "The Byzantine Background to the Italian Renaissance," *Proceedings of the American Philosophical Society* 100 (1956), 1–76.

14. K. Krumbacher, *Geschichte der byzantinischen Literatur*, 2nd ed. (Munich, 1897); L. Bréhier, *La civilisation byzantine* (Paris, 1950); A. A. Vasiliev, *History of the Byzantine Empire* (Madison, Wis., 1952), 713–722; J. Verpeaux, "Byzance et l'humanisme," *Bulletin de l'Association Guillaume Budé*, ser. 3, no. 3 (October 1952), 25–38.

15. M. De Wulf, *Histoire de la philosophie médiévale* (Louvain, 1934–1947), I (1934), 64–80, II (1936), 25–58 (these valuable sections by A. Pelzer have not been completely included in the American translation); G. Sarton, *Introduction to the History of Science*, 3 vols. (Baltimore, 1927–1948); J. T. Muckle, "Greek Works translated directly into Latin before 1350," *Mediaeval Studies*, IV (1942), 33–42, V (1943), 102–114; G. Lacombe and others, *Aristoteles Latinus*, I (Rome, 1939); E. Garin, "Le traduzioni umanistiche di Aristotele nel secolo XV," *Atti e Memorie dell 'Accademia Fiorentina di Scienze Morali 'La Colombaria'*, XVI (N.S. II, 1947–50), Florence, 1951, 55–104. See also: *Catalogus Translationum et Commentariorum* I (Washington, 1960), especially for the article by F. E. Cranz on Alexander of Aphrodisias.

15a. See now the detailed article on Juvenal commentaries by the late Eva M. Sanford, in: *Catalogus Translationum et Commentariorum* I (Washington, 1960).

16. Cf. the works of Gentile, Saitta, and Garin.

17. C. Lenient, *De Ciceroniano bello apud recentiores* (Paris, 1855); R. Sabbadini, *Storia del Ciceronianismo* (Turin, 1885); Th. Zielinski, *Cicero im Wandel der Jahrhunderte*, 3rd ed. (Leipzig, 1912); H. Baron, "Cicero and the Roman Civic Spirit in the Middle Ages and Early Renaissance," *Bulletin of the John Rylands Library*, XXII (1938), 72–97; W. Rüegg, *Cicero und der Humanismus;* Izora Scott, *Controversies over the Imitation of Cicero* (New York, 1910).

18. Alamanno Rinuccini, *Lettere ed Orazioni*, ed. V. R. Giustiniani (Florence, 1953), 97.

19. P. O. Kristeller, "Florentine Platonism and Its Relations with Humanism and Scholasticism," *Church History*, VIII (1939), 201–211.

20. G. Gentile, "Il concetto dell'uomo nel Rinascimento," in his *Il Pensiero italiano del Rinascimento*, 3rd ed. (Florence, 1940), 47–113; see below, Ch. 6.

21. Cf. "Du repentir," *Essais*, III, 2.

2. THE ARISTOTELIAN TRADITION

1. W. Jaeger, *Aristotle*, 2nd ed. (Oxford, 1948).

2. Cf. R. Klibansky, *The Continuity of the Platonic Tradition during the Middle Ages* (Oxford, 1939), 13.

3. B. Tatakis, *La philosophie byzantine* (E. Bréhier, *Histoire de la philos-*

ophie, deuxième fascicule supplémentaire, Paris, 1949). See above, ch. 1, n. 14.

4. M. Steinschneider, *Die Arabischen Uebersetzungen aus dem Griechischen* (*Beihefte zum centralblatt für Bibliothekswesen,* no. 5, Leipzig, 1890, 51-82; no. 12, 1893, 129-240); R. Walzer, "Arabic Transmission of Greek Thought to Medieval Europe," *Bulletin of the John Rylands Library,* XXIX (1945-1946), 160-183.

5. See ch. 1, n. 15. M. Steinschneider, "Die europäischen Übersetzungen aus dem Arabischen," *Sitzungsberichte der Kaiserlichen Akademie der Wissenschaften in Wien, Philosophisch-Historische Klasse,* vol. 149 (1904), no. 4, vol. 151 (1906), no. 1.

6. H. Rashdall, *The Universities of Europe, in the Middle Ages* (Oxford, 1936); H. Denifle and E. Chatelain, *Chartularium Universitatis Parisiensis,* 4 vols. (Paris, 1889-1897).

7. For some curious examples, see E. A. Moody, "Galileo and Avempace," *Journal of the History of Ideas,* XII (1951), 163-193, 375-422.

8. E. Renan, *Averroès et l'averroïsme,* 3rd ed. (Paris, 1867); P. Mandonnet, *Siger de Brabant et l'averroïsme latin au XIII e siècle,* 2nd ed. (Louvain, 1908-1911); F. Van Steenberghen, *Les oeuvres et la doctrine de Siger de Brabant* (Brussels, 1938); The same, *Siger de Brabant d'après ses oeuvres inédites,* 2 vols. (Louvain, 1931-1942); B. Nardi, *Sigieri di Brabante nel pensiero del Rinascimento italiano* (Rome, 1945); The same, "Averroismo," *Enciclopedia Cattolica,* II (Vatican City, 1949), 524-530; Anneliese Maier, "Eine italienische Averroistenschule aus der ersten Hälfte des 14. Jahrhunderts," in her *Die Vorläufer Galileis im 14. Jahrhundert* (Rome, 1949), 251-278; P. O. Kristeller, "Petrarch's 'Averroists,'" *Bibliothèque d'humanisme et Renaissance,* XIV (1952), 59-65.

9. Ricardo G. Villoslada, *La Universidad de Paris durante los estudios de Francisco de Vitoria* (Rome, 1938).

9a. William T. Costello, *The Scholastic Curriculum at Early Seventeenth-Century Cambridge.* Cambridge, Mass., 1958.

10. C. Giacon, *La seconda scolastica,* 3 vols. (Milan, 1944-1950).

11. P. Petersen, *Geschichte der Aristotelischen Philosophie im protestantischen Deutschland* (Leipzig, 1921); M. Wundt, *Die deutsche Schulmetaphysik des 17. Jahrhunderts* (Tübingen, 1939).

12. E. Gilson, *Etudes sur le rôle de la pensée médiévale dans la formation du système cartésien* (Paris, 1930); Matthias Meier, *Descartes und die Renaissance* (Münster, 1914); L. Blanchet, *Les antécédents historiques du 'Je pense, donc je suis,'* (Paris, 1920); H. A. Wolfson, *The Philosophy of Spinoza,* 2 vols. (Cambridge, Mass., 1934); J. Politella, *Platonism, Aristotelianism and Cabalism in the Philosophy of Leibniz* (Philadelphia, 1938).

13. Grabmann, *Mittelalterliches Geistesleben,* II (1936), 239-271; The same, "Gentile da Cingoli," *Sitzungsberichte der Bayerischen Akademie der Wissenschaften, Philosophisch-Historische Abteilung,* Jahrgang 1940 (Munich, 1941), no. 9; The same, "L'Aristotelismo italiano al tempo di Dante," *Rivista di filosofia neo-scolastica,* XXXVIII (1946), 260-277; B. Nardi, "L'averroismo bolognese nel secolo XIII e Taddeo Alderotto," *Rivista di storia della filosofia,* XXIII (1931), 504-517. Cf. n. 8 above. P. O. Kristeller "A Philosophical Treatise from Bologna Dedicated to Guido Cavalcanti," in *Medioevo e Rinascimento, Studi in Onore di Bruno Nardi* (Florence, 1955) I 425-463.

14. M. Clagett, *Giovanni Marliani and late medieval physics* (New York, 1941).

15. J. H. Randall, Jr., "The Development of Scientific Method in the School of Padua," *Journal of the History of Ideas,* I (1940), 177–206; E. Cassirer, *Das Erkenntnisproblem,* I (1922), 117ff.

16. F. Ehrle, *Der Sentenzenkommentar Peters von Candia* (Münster, 1925), 114ff; Villoslada, *La Universidad de Paris,* 279–307.

17. P. O. Kristeller, *Studies* (1956), 337–53.

18. In Francesco Patrizi's *Discussiones Peripateticae* (Basel, 1581).

19. This is quite apparent both from the manuscripts and from the commentaries.

20. Aristotle, *De arte poetica Guillelmo de Moerbeke interprete,* ed E. Valgimigli, E. Franceschini, and L. Minio-Paluello (*Aristoteles Latinus,* vol. XXXIII, Bruges-Paris, 1953).

21. J. E. Spingarn, *A History of Literary Criticism in the Renaissance,* 2nd ed. (New York, 1908); G. Toffanin, *La fine dell'umanesimo* (Turin, 1920).

22. For example, in the work of Ulisse Aldrovandi.

23. L. Zanta, *la renaissance du stoïcisme au XVI e siècle* (Paris, 1914); P. O. Kristeller, *Studies* (1956), 279–86; The same, "A New Manuscript Source for Pomponazzi's Theory of the Soul. . . ," *Revue Internationale de Philosophie,* vol. II, fasc. 2 (16 of series) (1951), 144–157; the same, "Two Unpublished Questions on the Soul by Pietro Pomponazzi," *Medievalia et Humanistica* IX (1955), 76–101; X (1956), 151; J. H. Randall in *The Renaissance Philosophy of Man* (Chicago, 1948), 257–279.

24. E. Garin, *Prosatori latini del Quattrocento* (Milan, 1952), 41ff (for Bruni); Q. Breen, "Giovanni Pico della Mirandola on the Conflict of Philosophy and Rhetoric. . . . ," *Journal of the History of Ideas,* XIII (1952), 384–426 (for Ermolao).

25. Paetow, ed., *The Battle of the Seven Arts;* L. Thorndike, *Science and Thought in the Fifteenth Century* (New York, 1929), 24–58; E. Garin, *La disputa delle arti nel Quattrocento* (Florence, 1947).

26. Perry Miller, *The New England Mind* (New York, 1939); Walter J. Ong, *Ramus: Method, and the Decay of Dialogue,* Cambridge, Mass., 1958; the same, *Ramus and Talon Inventory,* Cambridge, Mass., 1958.

27. In his *De tradendis disciplinis.*

28. P. O. Kristeller, "Florentine Platonism"; The same, "The Scholastic Background of Marsilio Ficino," *Studies* (1956), 35–97. E. Garin, *Giovanni Pico della Mirandola* (Florence, 1937); Avery Dulles, *Princeps Concordiae* (Cambridge, Mass., 1941); Q. Breen, "Giovanni Pico della Mirandola."

29. Cassirer, *Erkenntnisproblem,* I (1922).

30. Edward W. Strong, *Procedures and Metaphysics* (Berkeley, 1936).

31. Moody, "Galileo and Avempace."

32. A. Koyré, *Etudes Galiléennes,* 3 vols. (Paris, 1939).

3. RENAISSANCE PLATONISM

1. Alfred N. Whitehead, *Process and Reality* (New York, 1941; and Harper Torchbook, 1960), 63.

2. P. Merlan, *From Platonism to Neoplatonism* (The Hague, 1953).

3. H. Cherniss, *The Riddle of the Early Academy* (Berkeley, 1945).

4. W. Theiler, *Die Vorbereitung des Neuplatonismus* (Berlin, 1930).

5. J. Festugière, *La révélation d' Hermès Trismegiste,* 4 vols. (Paris, 1944–1954).

6. Proclus, *The Elements of Theology,* ed, and tr. E. R. Dodds (Oxford, 1933).

7. R. Klibansky, *The Continuity of the Platonic Tradition during the Middle Ages* (London, 1939 and 1950). This little book is the most important single, though not the only, source of this lecture down to the fifteenth century. Cf. also P. Shorey, *Platonism Ancient and Modern* (Berkeley, 1938).

8. See ch. 1, n. 14, and ch. 2, n. 3.

9. Milton V. Anastos, "Pletho's Calendar and Liturgy," *Dumbarton Oaks Papers* IV (1948), 183–305; F. Masai, *Pléthon et le Platonisme de Mistra* (Paris, 1956). For the conception of pagan theology, Plethon (and Ficino) were obviously indebted to Proclus. Cf. H. D. Saffrey, "Notes platoniciennes de Marsile Ficin dans un manuscrit de Proclus," *Bibliothèque d'Humanisme et Renaissance* XXI (1959), 161–184.

10. L. Mohler, *Kardinal Bessarion,* 3 vols. (Paderborn, 1923–1942).

11. See ch. 2, n. 4. F. Rosenthal, "On the Knowledge of Plato's Philosophy in the Islamic World," *Islamic Culture,* XIV (1940), 387–422.

12. G. Scholem, *Major Trends in Jewish Mysticism* (Jerusalem, 1941).

13. *De Civitate Dei,* VIII, 5 and 9ff, IX, 1, X, 1; P. Courcelle, *Recherches sur les Confessions de Saint Augustin* (Paris, 1950).

14. G. Théry, *Etudes Dionysiennes* (Paris, 1932–1937).

15. Toni Schmid, "Ein Timaioskommentar in Sigtuna," *Classica et Mediaevalia,* X (1948), 220–266.

16. E. Garin, "Una fonte ermetica poco nota," *La Rinascita,* vol. III, fasc. 12 (1940), 202–232.

17. Corpus Platonicum Medii Aevi: *Meno Interprete Henrico Aristippo,* ed. V. Kordeuter and C. Labowsky (London, 1940); *Phaedo interprete Henrico Aristippo,* ed. L. Minio-Paluello (London, 1950); *Parmenides . . . nec non Procli Commentarium in Parmenidem, pars ultima adhuc inedita interprete Guillelmo de Moerbeka,* ed. R. Klibansky and C. Labowsky (London, 1953).

18. A. Hyma, *The Christian Renaissance* (Grand Rapids, 1924).

19. Mohler, *Kardinal Bessarion.*

20. G. Gentile, "*Le traduzioni medievali di Platone e Francesco Petrarca,*" in his *Studi sul Rinascimento,* 2nd ed. (Florence, 1936), 23–88; L. Minio-Paluello, "Il Fedone latino con note autografe del Petrarca," *Accademia Nazionale dei Lincei, Rendiconti della Classe di Scienze morali, storiche e filologiche,* ser. VIII, vol. IV (1949), 107–113.

21. For a list of humanist versions of Plato, see P. O. Kristeller, *Supplementum Ficinianum,* I (Florence, 1937), p. clvi–clvii. For the versions of Bruni, see Leonardo Bruni Aretino, *Humanistisch-Philosophische Schriften,* ed. H. Baron (Leipzig-Berlin, 1928), 161, 163, 172–174; L. Bertalot, "Zur Bibliographie der Übersetzungen des Leonardus Brunus Aretinus," *Quellen und Forschungen aus italienischen Archiven und Bibliotheken,* XXVII (1937), 180–184. E. Garin, "Ricerche sulle traduzioni di Platone nella prima metà del sec. XV," in: *Medioevo e Rinascimento, Studi in onore di Bruno Nardi* (Florence, 1955) I 339–374. For Trapezuntius' version of the *Parmenides,* see R. Klibansky, "Plato's Parmenides in the Middle Ages and the

Renaissance," *Mediaeval and Renaissance Studies,* vol. I, pt. 2 (1943) 289–304.

22. E. Vansteenberghe, *Le Cardinal Nicolas de Cues* (Paris, 1920).

23. P. O. Kristeller, *The Philosophy of Marsilio Ficino* (New York, 1943); *Il pensiero filosofico di Marsilio Ficino* (Florence, 1953); G. Saitta, *Marsilio Ficino e la filosofia dell'umanesimo,* 3rd ed. (Bologna, 1954). M. Schiavone, *Problemi filosofici in Marsilio Ficino* (Milan, 1957); D. P. Walker, *Spiritual and Demonic Magic from Ficino to Campanella* (London, 1958).

24. E. Garin, *Giovanni Pico della Mirandola* (Florence, 1937); E. Anagnine, *G. Pico della Mirandola* (Bari, 1937).

25. Ioannes Picus, *Oratio de hominis dignitate,* in Latin and English (Lexington, Ky., 1953).

26. P. O. Kristeller, *Studies* (1956), 287–336; Nesca A. Robb, *Neoplatonism of the Italian Renaissance* (London, 1935).

27. S. Greenberg, *The Infinite in Giordano Bruno* (New York, 1950); Dorothy W. Singer, *Giordano Bruno* (New York, 1950); John C. Nelson, *Renaissance Theory of Love* (New York, 1958).

28. R. Marcel, "Les 'découvertes' d'Erasme en Angleterre," *Bibliothèque d'Humanisme et Renaissance,* XIV (1952) 117–123.

29. J. Hexter, *More's Utopia* (Princeton, 1952).

30. A. Renaudet, *Préréforme et Humanisme à Paris* (Paris, 1916).

31. Chr. Sigwart, *Ulrich Zwingli, Der Charakter seiner Theologie mit besonderer Rücksicht auf Picus von Mirandola dargestellt* (Stuttgart, 1855).

32. J. Blau, *The Christian Interpretation of the Cabala in the Renaissance* (New York, 1944).

33. Roy W. Battenhouse, "The Doctrine of Man in Calvin and in Renaissance Platonism," *Journal of the History of Ideas,* IX (1948), 447–471.

34. E. Massa, "L'anima e l'uomo in Egidio di Viterbo e nelle fonte classiche e medievali," *Testi Umanistici inediti sul 'De Anima' (Archivo di Filosofia,* Padua, 1951), 37–86.

35. J. D. Mansi, *Sacrorum Conciliorum Nova et Amplissima Collectio,* XXXII (Paris, 1902), 842–843.

36. W. Moench, *Die italienische Platonrenaissance und ihre Bedeutung für Frankreichs Literatur- und Geistesgeschichte* (Berlin, 1936). J. Festugière, *La philosophie de l'amour de Marsile Ficin et son influence sur la littérature française au XVI e siècle* (2nd ed., Paris, 1941).

37. Sears Jayne, "Ficino and the Platonism of the English Renaissance," *Comparative Literature,* IV (1952), 214–238.

38. Robb, *Neoplatonism of the Italian Renaissance,* 177ff; L. Tonelli, *L'amore nella poesia e nel pensiero del Rinascimento* (Florence, 1933); John C. Nelson, *Renaissance Theory of Love* (New York, 1958).

39. In his *Poetica,* a work of which I was able to discover extensive unpublished sections in a group of manuscripts (Parma, Biblioteca Palatina, cod. Pal. 408, 417, and 421).

40. P. O. Kristeller, "The Modern System of the Arts," *Journal of the History of Ideas,* XII (1951), 496–527, XIII (1952), 17–46.

41. E. Panofsky, *Idea* (Leipzig-Berlin, 1924).

42. E. H. Gombrich, "Botticelli's Mythologies," *Journal of the Warburg and Courtauld Institutes,* VIII (1945), 7–60; D. Redig de Campos, "Il concetto platonico-cristiano della Stanza della Segnatura," in his *Raffaello e Michel-*

angelo (Rome, 1946), 9–27; E. Panofsky, *Studies in Iconology* (New York, 1939), 171ff; A. Chastel, *Marsile Ficin et l'Art* (Paris, 1954).

43. O. Kinkeldey, "Franchino Gafori and Marsilio Ficino," *Harvard Library Bulletin*, I (1947), 379–382; P. O. Kristeller, *Studies* (1956), 451–70; D. P. Walker, *Spiritual and Demonic Magic*, p. 3ff.

44. Leonardo da Vinci's attitude towards humanism and Platonism has been a subject of controversy. For a more positive opinion, see now: A. Chastel, "Léonard et la culture," in *Léonard de Vinci et l'expérience scientifique au seizième siècle* (Paris, 1953), 251–263.

45. E. Cassirer, *Das Erkenntnisproblem* (Berlin, 1922); E. A. Burtt, *The Metaphysical Foundations of Modern Physical Science* (New York, 1951; and Anchor paperback, 1954).

46. B. Brickman, *An Introduction to Francesco Patrizi's Nova de Universis Philosophia* (New York, 1941).

47. Randall, "The Development of Scientific Method"; Moody, "Galileo and Avempace"; A. Koyré, "Galileo and Plato," *Journal of the History of Ideas*, IV (1943), 400–428; E. Cassirer, "Galileo's Platonism," *Studies and Essays in the History of Science and Learning in Honor of George Sarton* (New York, 1946), 279–297.

48. ". . . quando uno non sa la verità da per sè, è impossibile che altri glie ne faccia sapere . . . le vere (cose), cioè le necessarie, cioè quelle che è impossibile ad esser altrimenti, ogni mediocre discorso o le sa da sè o è impossibile che ei le sappia mai . . ."*Dialogo sopra i due massimi sistemi del mondo, Seconda giornata* in Galileo Galilei, *Le Opere*, VII (Florence, 1933), 183; Galileo Galilei, *Dialogue concerning the two chief world systems*, tr. S. Drake (Berkeley, 1953), 157–158; Galileo Galilei, *Dialogue on the Great World Systems*, tr. T. Salusbury, ed. G. de Santillana (Chicago, 1953), 172.

49. See ch. 2, n. 12.

50. E. Cassirer, *Die platonische Renaissance in England und die Schule von Cambridge* (Leipzig, 1932); *The Platonic Renaissance in England*, tr. J. P. Pettegrove (Austin, Tex., 1953).

4. PAGANISM AND CHRISTIANITY

1. Similar views on the Renaissance are still expressed by R. Niebuhr, *The Nature and Destiny of Man*, I (New York, 1941), 61ff, II (1943), 157ff.

2. J.-R. Charbonnel, *La pensée italienne au XVI e siècle et le courant libertin* (Paris, 1919).

3. P. O. Kristeller, "El Mito del Ateísmo Renacentista y la tradición francesa del librepensamiento," *Notas y Estudios de Filosofia*, vol. IV, fasc. 13 (1953), 1–14.

4. E. Walser, *Gesammelte Studien zur Geistesgeschichte der Renaissance* (Basel, 1952), especially 48–63: "Christentum und Antike in der Auffassung der italienischen Frührenaissance," and 96–128: "Studien zur Weltanschauung der Renaissance."

5. The term Pantheist was coined by John Toland in 1705 (*The Oxford English Dictionary*, VII [Oxford, 1933], 430).

6. Charbonnel, *La pensée italienne*.

7. A. Hyma, *The Christian Renaissance* (Grand Rapids, 1924).

8. This point is duly emphasized by Burckhardt (Part VI, ch. 2).

9. G. M. Monti, *Le confraternite medievali dell'alta e media Italia*, 2 vols. (Venice, 1927).

10. Wallace K. Ferguson, "The Revival of Classical Antiquity or the First Century of Humanism," The Canadian Historical Association, *Report of the Annual Meeting held at Ottawa*, June 12-15, 1957, pp. 13-30, at p. 24: ". . . it is sometimes necessary to point out that Christianity was not a medieval invention and that the Middle Ages have not had a monopoly of Christian faith."

11. K. Burdach, *Reformation, Renaissance, Humanismus*, 2nd ed. (Berlin-Leipzig, 1926).

12. G. Toffanin, *Storia dell'umanesimo; Che cosa fu l'umanesimo* (Florence, 1929); *History of Humanism* (tr. E. Gianturco, New York, 1954).

12a. See also S. A. Nulli, *Erasmo e il Rinascimento* (Turin, 1955), p. 445: ". . . parlare di *umanesimo cristiano* ha lo stesso senso che parlare di geometria cattolica o di chimica cristiana: è una cattiva espressione invece di dire: attività filologica e culturale esercitata da individui che si professano seguaci del cattolicismo circa argomenti che appartengono alla storia delle Chiese."

13. H.-I. Marrou, *Saint Augustin et la fin de la culture antique* (Paris, 1938); Renucci, *L'Aventure de l'Humanisme Européen au Moyen Age;* Martin R. P. McGuire, "Mediaeval Humanism," *The Catholic Historical Review*, XXXVIII (1953), 397-409.

14. Charles N. Cochrane, *Christianity and Classical Culture* (London, 1944; and Galaxy paperback, 1957), cf. my review in the *Journal of Philosophy*, XLI (1944), 576-581; Harry A. Wolfson, *Philo*, 2 vols. (Cambridge, Mass., 1947), cf. my review in the *Journal of Philosophy*, XLVI (1949), 359-363. One may also compare the manner in which E. Gilson *(Les Métamorphoses de la cité de Dieu* [Louvain-Paris, 1952], 6ff) tries to evade the obvious contribution of Stoicism to the notion of human solidarity.

15. M. Grabmann, *Die Geschichte der katholischen Theologie* (Freiburg, 1933), 15ff; J. De Ghellinck, *Le mouvement théologique du XIIe siècle*, 2nd ed. (Brussels-Paris, 1948); Artur M. Landgraf, *Einführung in die Geschichte der theologischen Literatur der Frühscholastik* (Regensburg, 1948).

16. P. O. Kristeller, *Studies* (1956), 355-72.

17. P. De Holhac, *Pétrarque et l'humanisme*, 2nd ed. (Paris, 1907).

18. Q. Breen, *John Calvin: A Study in French Humanism* (Grand Rapids, 1931); Paul Wernle, *Die Renaissance des Christentums im 16. Jahrhundert* (Tuebingen-Leipzig, 1904), who stresses this aspect especially in Erasmus and Zwingli.

19. Kristeller, *Studies* (1956), 355-72; P. Polman, *l'Element historique dans le controverse religieuse du XVIe siècle* (Gembloux, 1932).

20. U. Cassuto, *Gli Ebrei a Firenze nell 'età del rinascimento* (Florence, 1918), 275ff; S. Garofalo, "Gli umanisti italiani del secolo XV e la Bibbia," *Biblica*, XXVII (1946), 338-375; also in: *La Bibbia e il Concilio di Trento* (Rome, 1947), 38-75. Apart from the Vatican mss. cited by Garofalo, Manetti's version of the Psalms occurs also in two other contemporary mss., which shows that it attained a certain diffusion: Florence, Biblioteca Marucelliana, ms. C 336; Brussels, Bibliothèque Royale, ms. 10745.

21. Grabmann, *Die Geschiche der katholischen Theologie*, 155; L. von Pastor, *Geschichte der Päpste*, x (Freiburg, 1926), 147ff, 560ff.

22. Polman, *L'Elément historique*.

23. Grabmann, *Die Geschichte der katholischen Theologie*, 185ff. A. Siegmund, Die Ueberlieferung der griechischen christlichen Literatur in der lateinischen Kirche bis zum zwoelften Jahrhundert (Muenchen-Pasing, 1949).

24. Bruni, *Humanistisch-philosophische Schriften*, ed. H. Baron, 99f, 160f.

25. R. Sabbadini, *La scuola e gli studi di Guarino Guarini Veronese* (Catania, 1896), 138ff. See also the studies of W. H. Woodward.

26. Pastor, *Geschichte der Päpste*, x, 189; Polman, *L'Elément historique*, 392ff.

27. Polman, 539ff ("A la considérer dans son orientation historique, la controverse religieuse du XVI e siècle se rattache à l'humanisme"). E. Fueter (*Geschichte der neuren Historiographie* [Munich, 1911], 246ff) misses the problem by stating that humanism ignored the church, and that ecclesiastic historiography, as a child of the Reformation, was independent of humanism.

28. F. Seebohm, *The Oxford Reformers* (London, 1887); W. Dress, *Die Mystik des Marsilio Ficino* (Berlin-Leipzig, 1929); P. A. Duhamel, "The Oxford Lectures of John Colet," *Journal of the History of Ideas*, XIV (1953), 493–510.

29. Cf. "Augustine and the Early Renaissance."

30. See ch. 1, n. 3.

31. J. B. Bury, *The Idea of Progress* (London, 1920); Richard F. Jones, *Ancients and Moderns* (St. Louis, 1936).

32. J. Burckhardt, *Weltgeschichtliche Betrachtungen* (Leipzig, 1935), 10; *Force and Freedom*, tr. James H. Nichols (New York, 1943), 86.

33. ". . . duo praecipue paranda sunt arma, cui sit . . . cum universa vitiorum cohorte pugnandum . . . precatio et scientia . . . Sed precatio quidem potior, ut quae cum Deo sermones misceat, at scientia non minus necessaria tamen." (Desiderius Erasmus, "Enchiridion militis Christiani," 1503, in his *Ausgewählte Werke*, ed. H. and A. Holborn [Munich, 1933] 29).

5. HUMANISM AND SCHOLASTICISM IN THE ITALIAN RENAISSANCE

This article is based on a lecture given at Brown University on December 15, 1944. An Italian version of it appeared in *Humanitas* V 10, Oct., 1950, 988–1015.

1. *Die Cultur der Renaissance in Italien* (Basel, 1860; Eng. tr.: Harper Torchbooks, 1958).

2. For the controversy about the Renaissance, see H. Baron, "Renaissance in Italien," *Archiv für Kulturgeschichte*, XVII (1927), 226–52; XXI (1931), 95–119. J. Huizinga, "Das Problem der Renaissance," in his *Wege der Kulturgeschichte*, tr. W. Kaegi (Munich, 1930), 89–139. See also the discussion in the *Journal of the History of Ideas*, IV (1943), 1–74. See now: Wallace K. Ferguson, *The Renaissance in Historical Thought* (Boston, 1948).

3. K. Burdach, *Reformation, Renaissance, Humanismus*, 2nd ed. (Berlin-Leipzig, 1926); Wallace K. Ferguson, "Humanist Views of the Renaissance," *American Historical Review*, XLV (1939–40), 1–28. Id., *The Renaissance in*

Historical Thought, l. c., p. 1 ff. Herbert Weisinger, "The Self-Awareness of the Renaissance," *Papers of the Michigan Academy of Science, Arts, and Letters,* XXIX (1944), 561–67. Id., "Who began the Revival of Learning," *ibid.,* XXX (1945), 625–38; Id., "Renaissance Accounts of the Revival of Learning," *Studies in Philology,* XLV (1948), 105–18; Id., "The Renaissance Theory of the Reaction against the Middle Ages . . . ," *Speculum,* XX (1945), 461–67; Id., "Ideas of History during the Renaissance," *Journal of the History of Ideas,* VI (1945), 415–35; F. Simone, *La coscienza della Rinascita negli Umanisti francesi* (Rome, 1949); E. Garin, "Umanesimo e Rinascimento," in *Problemi ed orientamenti critici di lingua e di letteratura italiana,* ed. A. Momigliano, vol. III: *Questioni e correnti di storia letteraria* (Milan, 1949), 349–404. Most of the passages quoted by these scholars are later than the beginning of the fifteenth century. Yet Frate Guido da Pisa in his commentary on Dante wrote as early as 1330: "Per istum enim poetam resuscitata est mortua poesis . . . Ipse vero poeticam scientiam suscitavit et antiquos poetas in mentibus nostris reviviscere fecit" (O. Bacci, *La Critica letteraria* [Milan, 1910], p. 163).

4. Burdach's attempts to derive the concept of the Renaissance from religious or mystical traditions no longer convince me. However, a Carolingian poet has the following line: "Aurea Roma iterum renovata renascitur orbi" (E. K. Rand, "Renaissance, why not?" *Renaissance,* I [1943], p. 34). Milo Crispinus says in his biography of Lanfranc: "quem Latinitas in antiquum scientiae statum ab eo restituta tota supremum debito cum amore agnoscit magistrum." (Migne, *P.L.,* CL, 29). For the political aspect of the conception, see P. E. Schramm, *Kaiser, Rom und Renovatio,* 2 vols. (Leipzig, 1929). See also Augustine's judgment on Ambrose *(Soliloquia,* II, 14, 26): "ille in quo ipsam eloquentiam quam mortuam dolebamus perfectam revixisse cognovimus."

5. E. Panofsky, "Renaissance and Renascences," *Kenyon Review,* VI (1944), 201–36.

6. E. Gilson, "Humanisme médiéval et Renaissance," in his *Les Idées et les lettres* (Paris, 1932), 171–96. E. R. Curtius, *Europaeische Literatur und Lateinisches Mittelalter* (Bern, 1948), pp. 41ff. and 387ff. (Eng. tr., New York, 1953).

7. The isolation of Italy in the Middle Ages and the comparative scantiness of Italian antecedents for Dante has been noted by K. Vossler, *Mediaeval Culture,* tr. W, C, Lawton (New York, 1929, 1960), II, 4ff. *Die Göttliche Komödie,* v. II, pt. I (Heidelberg, 1908), pp. 582ff.

8. There are notable exceptions, such as Guido of Arezzo, Alfanus of Salerno, and Henricus of Settimello, but they do not change the general picture. For the share of Italy in medieval Latin culture prior to the thirteenth century, see F. Novati and A. Monteverdi, *Le Origini* (Milan, 1926); A. Viscardi, *Le Origini* (Milan, 1939); M. Manitius, *Geschichte der lateinischen Literatur des Mittelalters,* 3 vols. (Munich, 1911–31).

9. Although several of the most famous representatives of scholastic theology were Italians, such as Lanfranc, Anselm, Peter Lombard, Thomas Aquinas, and Bonaventura, they did most of their studying and teaching in France. For Lanfranc, see F. Novati, "Rapports littéraires de l'Italie et de la France au XI siècle," *Académie des Inscriptions et Belles-Lettres,Comptes Rendus des Séances de l'année 1910,* pp. 169–84. A typical representative of

Italian theology in the eleventh century was Peter Damiani, and his background was juristic and rhetorical rather than philosophical; see J. A. Endres, *Petrus Damiani und die weltliche Wissenchaft* (Münster, 1910).

10. For the history of education in Italy, see G. Manacorda, *Storia della scuola in Italia,* 2 pts. (Milan, n. d.). Typical representatives of Italian rhetoric in the tenth and eleventh century are Gunzo of Novara and Anselm the Peripatetic. It should be noted that the library of Bobbio in the tenth century was rich in grammatical treatises, but possessed few classical poets (G. Becker, *Catalogi Bibliothecarum antiqui* [Bonn, 1885], 64ff).

11. Ch. H. Haskins, *The Renaissance of the Twelfth Century* (Cambridge, Mass., 1927; also Meridian paperback, 1958). For secular eloquence, see below.

12. For French influences in the thirteenth century, see G. Bertoni, *Il Duecento,* 3rd ed. (Milan, 1939). Many poems and prose works by Italian authors were written in French, and much of the early vernacular poetry and prose in Italian is derived from French models.

13. After having praised Dante and Petrarch as the restorers of poetry, Boccaccio continues: "inspice quo Romanum corruerit imperium . . . quid insuper philosophorum celebres titulos et poetarum myrthea laureaque serta meditari . . . quid in memoriam revocare militarem disciplinam . . . quid legum auctoritatem . . . quid morum conspicuum specimen. Haec omnia . . . una cum Italia reliqua et libertate caelesti a maioribus nostris . . . neglecta sunt a nationibus exteris aut sublata aut turpi conquinata labe sordescunt . . . et si omnia resarciri nequeant, hoc saltem poetici nominis fulgore . . . inter barbaras nationes Roma saltem aliquid veteris maiestatis possit ostendere" (letter to Jacopo Pizzinghe, in: *Le lettere edite e inedite di Messer Giovanni Boccaccio,* ed. F. Corazzini [Florence, 1877], p. 197). See K. Burdach, *Rienzo und die geistige Wandlung seiner Zeit* (Berlin, 1913–28), pp. 510f. Also Salutati, in his letter to Peter of Mantua, after admitting that Rome now has lost her military power, says that there is no excuse for her being excelled by other nations in literary distinction. "Gaudebam igitur apud nos emergere qui barbaris illis quondam gentibus saltem in hoc palmam eriperet, qualem me tibi (read: te mihi) fama et multorum relatio promittit," alluding to the achievements of Peter of Mantua in the field of logic *(Epistolario di Coluccio Salutati,* ed. F. Novati, III [Rome, 1896], 319f).

14. For the classical studies of the humanists, see G. Voigt, *Die Wiederbelebung des classischen Alterthums,* 3rd ed. (Berlin, 1893), II, 373f.; Sir J. E. Sandys, *A History of Classical Scholarship,* II (Cambridge, 1908), pp. 1ff.

15. These discoveries included Lucretius, Tacitus, Manilius, several plays of Plautus, and several orations and rhetorical works of Cicero. See R. Sabbadini. *Le scoperte dei codici latini e greci ne' secoli XIV e XV,* 2 vols. (Florence, 1905–14); M. Manitius, *Handschriften antiker Autoren in mittelalterlichen Bibliothekskatalogen* (Leipzig, 1935).

16. It is not generally realized that fifteenth century manuscripts of the Latin classics are probably more numerous than those of all previous centuries taken together. These manuscripts are despised by most modern editors, and their value for establishing a critical text may be small. However, their existence is an important phenomenon since it reflects the wide diffusion of the classical authors during the Renaissance.

17. Louise R. Loomis, *Medieval Hellenism* (Lancaster, Pa., 1906).

18. For the translations of the twelfth century, see Ch. H. Haskins, *Studies in the History of Mediaeval Science,* 2nd ed. (Cambridge, Mass., 1927). For the thirteenth century, see M. De Wulf, *Histoire de la philosophie médiévale,* 6th ed., II (Louvain, 1936). A bibliography of Latin translations from the Greek is still a major desideratum, even though some partial contributions have been made recently. See esp. J. T. Muckle, "Greek Works translated directly into Latin before 1350," *Mediaeval Studies,* IV (1942), 33–42; V (1943), 102–14. A more comprehensive biobliography is now being prepared by a group of scholars. For the study of Greek in the Middle Ages, see now the articles of R. Weiss, cited above, art. 3.

19. For the study of Greek classical literature in medieval Constantinople, see K. Krumbacher, *Geschichte der byzantinischen Literatur,* 2nd ed. (Munich, 1897), 499ff. The direct influence of this Byzantine tradition on the Greek studies of the Italian humanists is beyond any question. There may also have been some indirect Byzantine influence on the Latin studies of the humanists. The range of interest of the humanists resembles that of many Byzantine scholars.

20. For the literary production of the humanists, see Voigt, *op. cit.,* 11, 394ff., V. Rossi, *Il Quattrocento,* 2nd ed. (Milan, 1933).

21. The link between the humanists and the medieval rhetoricians has been recognized only by very few scholars, such as F. Novati, H. Wieruszowski, and E. Kantorowicz. These scholars, however, chiefly noticed that the medieval rhetoricians show some of the personal characteristics commonly attributed to the humanists. I should like to go further and to assume a direct professional and literary connection of which the personal similarities are merely a symptom. The common opinion is quite different, and most historians speak of the *ars dictaminis* as if there were no humanist rhetoric, and viceversa. See below.

22. For the contributions of the humanists to philosophy, see: F. Ueberweg, *Grundriss der Geschichte der Philosophie,* III, 12th ed. (Berlin, 1924), 6ff.; G. De Ruggiero, *Storia della filosofia,* pt. 3, 2nd ed., 2 vols. (Bari, 1937); G. Gentile, *La filosofia* (Milan, n. d.); E. Cassirer, *Individuum und Kosmos in der Philosophie der Renaissance* (Berlin-Leipzig, 1927). For further literature on the entire subject of Renaissance philosophy, see P. O. Kristeller and J. H. Randall Jr., "The Study of the Philosophies of the Renaissance," *Journal of the History of Ideas,* II (1941), 449–96. E. Garin, *La filosofia,* I (Milan, 1947), pp. 169–274; Id., *Der italienische Humanismus* (Bern, 1947); Id., *Filosofi italiani del Quattrocento* (Florence, 1942); C. Carbonaro, *Il secolo XV* (Milan, 1943); G. Saitta, *Il pensiero italiano nell'umanesimo e nel rinascimento,* vol. I: *L'Umanesimo* (Bologna, 1949).

22a. This statement does not mean, as E. Garin implies *(Giornale Critico,* 1952, p. 99) that I deny the philosophical significance of the Renaissance period; see above, art. 3.

22b. This point has been rightly indicated by R. McKeon, "Renaissance and Method in Philosophy," *Studies in the History of Ideas,* III (1935), 37–114. "That shift in the emphasis in the three arts, that subversion of dialectic to grammar, is in itself sufficient to account for the changes which the Renaissance is reputed to have made." (*l. c.,* p. 87). I am not convinced by McKeon's attempt to distinguish within the Renaissance, as two separate trends, an emphasis on grammar represented by Erasmus, and one on rhetoric represented by Nizolius. The grammatical character of early Italian humanism and its rise before the time of Petrarch have been illustrated in the recent studies of R. Weiss: *The Dawn of Humanism in Italy* (London, 1947); "Lineamenti per una storia del primo umanesimo fiorentino," *Rivista storica italiana*, LX (1948), 349–66; *Il primo secolo dell'umanesimo* (Rome, 1949).

23. For Pico's defense of the medieval philosophers against Ermolao Barbaro, see my article, "Florentine Platonism and its Relations with Humanism and Scholasticism," *Church History*, VIII (1939), 203f. Q. Breen, "Giovanni Pico della Mirandola on the Conflict of Philosophy and Rhetoric," *Journal of the History of Ideas*, XIII (1952), 384–426. For Alciato's defense of the medieval jurists against Valla, see R. Sabbadini, *Storia del Ciceronianismo* (Turin, 1885), pp. 88–92; B. Brugi, *Per la storia della giurisprudenza e delle università italiane, Nuovi saggi* (Turin, 1921), pp. 111ff.

24. This humanist logic is represented by Valla, Agricola, Nizolius, and Ramus. For Nizolius, see R. McKeon, "Renaissance and Method in Philosophy," *Studies in the History of Ideas*, III (1935), 105ff. For Ramus, see Perry Miller, *The New England Mind* (New York, 1939), pp. 154ff.

25. For the battle of the arts, see *The Battle of the Seven Arts . . . by Henri d'Andeli*, ed. L. J. Paetow (Berkeley, 1914). There was a rivalry between medicine and law, in which the humanists were not directly concerned at all. See L. Thorndike, "Medicine versus Law at Florence" in his *Science and Thought in the Fifteenth Century* (New York, 1929), 24–58. Behind this kind of literature is the rivalry of the various faculties and sciences at the universities, a rivalry that found its expression in the opening lectures delivered every year by each professor in praise of his own field. One such lecture by the humanist Philippus Beroaldus senior, professor at Bologna, is entitled "Declamatio philosophi, medici et oratoris" (in his *Varia Opuscula* [Basel, 1513]). Of course, the prize is given to the orator. See now Coluccio Salutati, *De nobilitate legum et medicinae*, ed. E. Garin (Florence, 1947), p. XLVI ff. E. Garin, *La Disputa delle Arti nel Quattrocento* (Florence, 1947).

26. J. Burckhardt, *Die Kultur der Renaissance in Italien*, 13th ed. (Stuttgart, 1921), p. 151. (Eng. tr. *op. cit.*).

27. For the careers of the humanists, see the works of Voigt and Rossi.

28. For the connection of Salutati with the medieval tradition of the *Ars dictaminis* and *Ars notaria*, see F. Novati, *La giovinezza di Coluccio Salutati* (Turin, 1888), pp. 66ff. This chapter was reprinted with important omissions in his *Freschi e minii del Dugento* (Milan, 1908), pp. 299–328. There is at Naples a manuscript of the early fifteenth century transcribed for a young student of rhetoric, which contains the letters of Petrus de Vineis, together with those of Salutati, and of the latter's contemporary Pellegrino Zambeccari (L. Frati, "L'epistolario inedito di Pellegrino Zambeccari," *Atti e Memorie della R. Deputazione di Storia patria per le provincie di Romagna*, Ser. IV, vol. XIII (1923), pp. 169ff.) Another manuscript with the same content is in the Hague (*Epistolario di Pellegrino Zambeccari*, ed. L. Frati (Rome, 1929), pp. XVIIff.). I am indebted for this information to Ludwig Bertalot. Although Burdach's attempt to make of Cola di Rienzo the central figure of the Italian Renaissance must be rejected, it should be noticed that Cola was a notary by profession and owed a good deal of his reputation to

the style of his letters and speeches. Burdach, who emphasizes the influence of Joachimite ideas on Cola, fails to meet the objection that Cola became familiar with these ideas only after his flight from Rome *(Rienzo und die geistige Wandlung seiner Zeit* [Berlin, 1923-28], p. 10).

29. For the literary production of the humanists, see the works of Voigt and Rossi. For their historiography, see E. Fueter, *Geschichte der neueren Historiographie,* 3rd ed. (Munich, 1936).

30. For the grammatical studies of the humanists in their relation to the Middle Ages, see R. Sabbadini, *La scuola e gli studi di Guarino Guarini Veronese* (Catania, 1896), pp. 38ff.

31. There are many humanist treatises on epistolography, and many collections of "salutations" in humanist manuscripts. The letters of most major humanists were collected and reprinted primarily as models for literary imitation.

32. Ch. S. Baldwin, *Medieval Rhetoric and Poetic* (New York, 1928), pp. 206ff. and 228ff. especially p. 230; R. McKeon, "Rhetoric in the Middle Ages," *Speculum,* XVII (1942), 27f. For the *Ars dictaminis* in Italy, especially during the twelfth century, see Ch. H. Haskins, *Studies in Medieval Culture,* (Oxford, 1929), 170–92. See also: E. Kantorowicz, "An 'Autobiography' of Guido Faba," *Medieval and Renaissance Studies,* I, 2 (1943), 253–80. The same, "Anonymi 'Aurea Gemma',", *Medievalia et Humanistica,* I (1943), 41–57. Helene Wieruszowski, "Ars dictaminis in the Time of Dante," *ibid.,* 95–108. For the *Ars praedicandi,* see H. Caplan, *Medieval Artes Praedicandi,* 2 vols. (Ithaca, N. Y., 1934-36); Th. M. Charland, *Artes Praedicandi* (Paris-Ottawa, 1936). Italy's contribution to the literature on preaching seems to have been small and belated.

33. Voigt, *op. cit.,* II, 436ff. Ch. S. Baldwin, *Renaissance Literary Theory and Practice* (New York, 1939), p. 39ff. For a typical collection of humanist orations, see L. Bertalot, "Eine Sammlung Paduaner Reden des XV. Jahrhunderts," *Quellen und Forschungen aus italienischen Archiven und Bibliotheken* XXVI (1936), 245–67.

34. See the studies of E. Kantorowicz and H. Wieruszowski, and especially A. Galletti, *L'eloquenza* (Milan, 1904–38), pp. 430ff.

35. Galletti, *loc. cit.*

36. Some of the rhetorical treatises and models of the thirteenth century are discussed by Galletti, *op. cit.,* 454ff. Guido Faba's *Parlamenti ed epistole* (ed. A. Gaudenzi, *I suoni, le forme e le parole dell'odierno dialetto della città di Bologna* [Turin, 1889]), include several model speeches. Models for political and funeral speeches are inserted in the anonymous "Oculus Pastoralis" and in other treatises written for the instruction of city officials (F. Hertter, *Die Podestàliteratur Italiens im 12. und 13. Jahrhundert,* Leipzig-Berlin, 1910). For an example of early academic oratory, see H. Kantorowicz, "The Poetical Sermon of a Mediaeval Jurist," *Journal of the Warburg Institute,* II (1938–39), 22–41. For the speech of an ambassador, see G. L. Haskins and E. Kantorowicz, "A Diplomatic Mission of Francis Accursius and his Oration before Pope Nicholas III," *English Historical Review,* LVIII (1943), 424–47. The medieval legal background of the wedding speeches of the humanists has been studied by F. Brandileone, *Saggi sulla storia della celebrazione del matrimonio in Italia* (Milan, 1906), but he does not mention any pre-humanistic wedding speeches. Rhetorical rules and samples are in-

cluded in some of the early instructions for advocates; see M. A. von Beth-mann-Hollweg, *Der Civilprozess des gemeinen Rechts in geschichtlicher Entwicklung, VI* (Bonn, 1874), pp. 148–59. Boñcompagno's *Rhetorica Novissima* (ed. A. Gaudenzi, *Bibliotheca iuridica medii aevi,* II [Bologna, 1892]) is not a treatise on *dictamen,* as most scholars seem to assume, but a rhetorical instruction for advocates. Also the treatise of Jacques de Dinant, published by A. Wilmart, *Analecta Reginensia* (Vatican City, 1933), pp. 113–51, covers judicial oratory. It is often asserted that the humanists did not cultivate judicial oratory (Rossi, 154), yet this is contradicted by a passage of Jovious (Burckhardt, 176), and there are at least a few examples of judicial speeches composed by humanists (Leonardo Bruni Aretino, *Humanistisch-Philosophische Schriften,* ed. Baron [Leipzig, 1928], p. 179; J. Paquier, *De Philippi Beroaldi Junioris vita et scriptis* [Paris, 1900], pp. 96–113). A systematic investigation of the various types of humanist oratory and of their medieval antecedents has not yet been undertaken. It ought to include a study of the mutual relations between sacred and secular eloquence, and of possible Byzantine influences. See Krumbacher, 454ff. and 470ff. I hope to return to this subject in a separate article. The legal background of the wedding orations appears sometimes in their titles, e.g., "contractus matrimonialis compillatus per Manfredum de Justis Veronensem" (cod. Laur. Ashb. 271, cfr. C. Paoli, *I codici Ashburnhamiani della R. Biblioteca Mediceo-Laurenziana di Firenze* [Rome, 1887-1917], p. 296 n. 195); "contractus Guarini Veronensis pro comite Jacopino" (Ricc. 421 f. 43). The title of another form speech shows that also Pico's famous oration belonged to an established formal type: "ad colligendos audientium animos in disputatione fienda" (Ricc. 421 f. 28).

37. Fueter fails to discuss the relations between medieval and humanistic historiography.

38. I should like to mention Carolus Sigonius for his masterful discussion of the forged charter of Theodosius II for Bologna university *(Opera Omnia,* VI (Milan, 1787), pp. 985 ff.). His remark on the task of history, made in connection with the donation of Constantine, is a quotation from Cicero: "primam legem historiae esse ut ne quid falsi audeat, ne quid veri non audeat" *(ibid.,* p. 985, cf. *De Oratore,* II, 15, 62).

39. For example, Boncompagno of Signa *(Liber de obsidione Anconae,* ed. G. C. Zimolo [Bologna, 1937]) and Rolandinus of Padua *(Cronica,* ed. A. Bonardi [Città di Castello, 1905-08]).

40. G. Bertoni, *Il Duecento,* p. 263. Machiavelli was on the payroll of the university of Pisa for writing his Florentine history.

41. Allan H. Gilbert, *Machiavelli's Prince and its Forerunners* (Durham, N. C., 1938). The question *De nobilitate,* dear to the humanists of the fifteenth century, was already discussed in the thirteenth (G. Bertoni, "Una lettera amatoria di Pier della Vigna," *Giornale storico della letteratura italiana, LVIII* [1911], p. 33ff.). The humanist treatises on the dignity and happiness of man also continued medieval discussions (G. Gentile, "Il concetto dell'uomo nel Rinascimento," in his *Il pensiero italiano del rinascimento,* 3rd ed. [Florence, 1940], pp. 47–113).

42. Boncompagno of Signa wrote two moral treatises: *Amicitia* (ed. Sarina Nathan [Rome, 1909], and *De malo senectutis et senii* (ed. F. Novati, *Rendiconti della Reale Accademia dei Lincei, Classe di Scienze Morali, Storiche e Filologiche,* Ser. V, vol. I [1892], pp. 50–59).

43. Novati-Monteverdi, *Le Origini;* F. Novati, *L'influsso del pensiero latino sopra la civiltà italiana nel Medio Evo,* 2nd ed. (Milan, 1899); U. Ronca, *Cultura medioevale e poesia latina d'Italia nei secoli XI e XII,* 2 vols. (Rome, 1892); F. J. E. Raby, *A History of Secular Latin Poetry in the Middle Ages,* 2 vols. (Oxford, 1934).

44. The rise of Latin poetry in Italy begins with the Paduan group of "pre-humanists," see G. Bertoni, *Il Duecento,* pp. 272ff.; N. Sapegno, *Il Trecento* (Milan, 1934), pp. 149ff.

45. A comprehensive study of the literature of medieval and Renaissance commentaries on the classical authors is a major desideratum. Much scattered information may be found concerning the commentaries on individual authors. The commentaries written before 1200 are listed in Manitius, *op. cit.* An interesting survey of such commentaries up to 1300, by B. H. (Hauréau), is hidden in the *Histoire littéraire de la France,* XXIX (1885) 568–83. Hauréau lists only one commentary which he believes to be from Italy. Of Italian origin are also certain legal glosses on Seneca, written in the twelfth century (C. Pascal, *Letteratura latina medievale* [Catania, 1909], pp. 150–54). There are also some Italian commentaries on Martianus Capella, but this refers to the teaching of the "artes" rather than that of the "authores." The Paduans began to study Seneca's tragedies, and after the end of the thirteenth century, the number of classical commentaries begins to increase. That these early Italian commentators were acquainted with the work of their French predecessors has been shown in the case of Giovanni del Virgilio by F. Ghisalberti ("Giovanni del Virgilio espositore delle 'Metamorfosi'," *Giornale Dantesco* XXXIV [1933], 31ff.). Relations between medieval and humanistic commentaries are also noticed by Eva M. Sanford ("The manuscripts of Lucan: Accessus and Marginalia," *Speculum* IX [1934], pp. 278–95). For the history and form of medieval commentaries, see now: E. A. Quain, "The Medieval Accessus ad auctores," *Traditio* III (1945), 215–64; R. W. Hunt, "The Introductions to the 'Artes' in the Twelfth Century," *Studia Mediaevalia in honorem admodum Reverendi Patris Raymundi Josephi Martin* (Brugis, c. 1949), 85–112; R. B. C. Huygens, "Accessus ad Auctores," *Latomus* XII (1953), 296–311; 460–84. Cf. also L. Bertalot, *Deutsche Literaturzeitung* XXXII (1911), 3166–69. An important exception which seems to deserve further study is the ms. 404 of the Pierpont Morgan Library in New York which was written in Italy in the twelfth century and contains the complete works of Horace with early glosses *(Italian Manuscripts in the Pierpont Morgan Library,* by Meta Harrsen and George K. Boyce [New York, 1953], p. 6, no. 7). The dating of the manuscript has been confirmed to me by Prof. Luisa Banti.

46. See Sabbadini, *Le scoperte.*

47. A. Clerval, *Les écoles de Chartres au moyen âge* (Paris, 1895); L. Delisle, "Les écoles d'Orléans au douzième et au treizième siècle," *Annuaire-Bulletin de la Société de l'histoire de France,* VII (1869), 139–54. See also Paetow, *The Battle of the Seven Arts.* For the contrast of "artes" and "authores," see E. Norden, *Die antike Kumstprosa,* II, Leipzig, 1898, pp. 688ff. and 724ff. To the well known material on the study of the "authores" in medieval France, I should like to add the following passage from the chronist Landulphus Junior, which seems to have remained unnoticed: "revocare Yordanum de Clivi a provincia que dicitur Sancti Egidii in qua ipse

Yordanus legebat lectionem auctorum non divinorum sed paganorum" (*Historia Mediolamensis,* ed. C. Castiglioni, Bologna, 1934, p. 18). The event must be dated shortly after 1100 A. D.

48. Perhaps the earliest dated evidence of the reading of classical authors in an Italian school of the Middle Ages is the criminal record of the theft of "three books of Ovid" from a teacher of grammer in Bologna (1294), see O. Mazzoni Toselli, *Racconti storici estratti dall'archivio criminale di Bologna,* III, (Bologna, 1870), 39f.

49. In 1321, Giovanni del Virgilio was appointed to lecture at Bologna on versification and on Virgil, Statius, Lucan, and Ovid (Ghisalberti, *loc. cit.,* 4f.). L. J. Paetow comments on this document as follows: "This was a good beginning . . . but the fair promise had no fulfillment" (*The Arts Course at Medieval Universities,* Urbana-Champaign, 1910, p. 60). Actually, the promise did find its fulfillment in the development of Italian humanism. The teaching of the classical authors never ceased in Italy after that memorable date which coincides with the approximate time when Petrarch was a student at Bologna.

50. For French influences on Italian humanism in the fourteenth century, see also B. L. Ullman, "Some Aspects of the Origin of Italian Humanism," *Philological Quarterly,* XX, 1941, 20–31.

51. Burckhardt, *op. cit.,* p. 154.

52. K. Vossler, *Poetische Theorien in der italienischen Frührenaissance,* Berlin, 1900.

53. The work by V. Lancetti, *Memorie intorno ai poeti laureati d'ogni tempo e d'ogni nazione* (Milan, 1839), is antiquated, but has not been replaced. Important contributions were made by F. Novati, "La suprema aspirazione di Dante," in his *Indagini e postille dantesche,* Bologna, 1899, p. 83ff., and by E. H. Wilkins, "The Coronation of Petrarch," *Speculum,* XVIII, 1943, pp. 155–97. I believe that the coronation ceremony developed from the public recitals and approbations of books at the medieval universities (on such approbations, see L. Thorndike, "Public Readings of New Works in Mediaeval Universities," *Speculum,* I, 1926, pp. 101–3, and the additional notes by Haskins and Thorndike, *ibid.,* pp. 221 and 445ff.). The intermediary link is the coronation of the approved book, as in the case of Boncompagno at Bologna 1215 (Novati, *Indagini,* p. 86f.). There is definite evidence that Mussato was crowned not only for his tragedy *Ecerinis,* but also for his historical work on Henry VII. Also the diploma of Petrarch's coronation refers to him repeatedly as a poet and historian (*Opera Omnia,* Basel, 1581, IV, 6–7), and there are later cases of persons crowned as poets and orators.

54. Petrarch was examined by King Robert of Naples and took the king's testimonial letters to Rome, that is, followed much of the procedure that was used for academic degrees in the kingdom of Naples. His diploma resembles doctoral diplomas and grants him the authorization "tam in dicta arte poetica quam in dicta historica arte . . . legendi, disputandi atque interpretandi veterum scripturas et novas (read: novos) a seipso . . . libros et poemata componendi . . ." (*loc. cit.*).

55. The chair of moral philosophy was held, for example, by Barzizza and by Filelfo.

56. Lectures on the Greek or Latin text of Aristotle and other philosophical authors were given at Florence by Marsuppini, Argyropulos, and Politian,

at Bologna by Codrus Urceus, and at Padua by Leonicus Thomaeus. I expect
to treat this subject in a future study of the Italian universities.

57. On *humanitas* in Roman antiquity, see W. Jaeger, *Humanism and
Theology*, Milwaukee, 1943, pp. 20ff. and 72f. M. Schneidewin, *Die antike
Humanitaet*, Berlin, 1897, *pp.* 31ff.; R. Reitzenstein, *Werden und Wesen der
Humanität*, Strassburg, 1907; I. Heinemann, "Humanitas," in Pauly-Wissowa,
Real-Encyclopaedie der classischen Altertumswissenschaft, Supplementband
V, 1931, col. 282–310; J. Niedermann, *Kultur*, Florence, 1941, pp. 29ff.

58. The clearest statement is found in the famous library canon composed by Nicholas V in his youth for Cosimo de' Medici. After having listed
many books on theology, then the works of Aristotle in logicis, in physicis,
in metaphysica, and in moralibus, the Arabic and Greek commentators on
Aristotle, other philosophical works translated from the Greek, and works
on mathematics, he continued as follows: "de studiis autem humanitatis quan-
tum ad grammaticam, rhetoricam, historicam et poeticam spectat ac mo-
ralem . . ." (G. Sforza, "La patria, la famiglia ed i parenti di papa
Niccolò V," *Atti della Reale Accademia Lucchese di Scienze, Lettere ed Arti*,
XXIII, 1884, p. 380). An educational charter of the Jesuits of 1591 speaks
of "studia humanitatis, hoc est grammaticae, historiae, poeticae et rhetoricae"
(quoted by K. Borinski, *Die Antike in Poetik und Kumsttheorie*, II, Leipzig,
1924, p. 327). Pierre Bersuire calls Petrarch "poetam utique et oratorem
egregium in omni morali philosophia nec non et historica et poetica disciplina
eruditum" (F. Ghisalberti, "L'Ovidius moralizatus di Pierre Bersuire," *Studi
Romanzi*, XXIII, 1933, p. 90). After Leonardo Bruni's death, according to
his epitaph in S. Croce, "historia luget, eloquentia muta est, Ferturque Musas
tum Graecas tum Latinas lacrimas tenere non potuisse." Peter Luder an-
nounced at Heidelberg in 1456 public courses on "studia humanitatis id est
poetarum oratorum ac hystoriographorum libros," and at Leipzig in 1462 on
"studia humanitatis, hystoriographos, oratores scilicet et poetas" (L. Bertalot,
"Humanistische Vorlesungsankündigungen in Deutschland im 15. Jahrhundert," *Zeitschrift für Geschichte der Erziehung und des Unterrichts* V
1915, pp. 3–4). G. Sforza's manuscript source for the "Inventarium Nicolai
pape V quod ipse composuit ad instantiam Cosme de Medicis ut ab ipso
Cosma audivi die XII novembr. 1463 ego frater Leonardus Ser Uberti de
Florentia O. P. presente R. o patre fratre Sante de Florentia priore Sancti
Marci Flor(entini) eiusdem ord(inis)" is cod. Conv. Soppressi J VII 30
(S. Marco) of the Biblioteca Nazionale in Florence, f. 180–185v (the reference given by Sforza, l. c., p. 359, is misleading). Characteristic is also the
title of one of Filelfo's orations: "oratio de laudibus historie poetice philo-
sophie et que hasce complectitur eloquentie" (cod. Vallicell. F. 20 f. 213v).

59. This was attempted, however, in the sixteenth century by Vives in his
work *De tradendis disciplinis*.

60. The humanist Leonardo Bruni, when comparing Dante and Petrarch,
attributes greater knowledge in philosophy and mathematics to Dante,
"perocchè nella scienza delle lettere e nella cognizione della lingua latina
Dante fu molto inferiore al Petrarca" (*Le Vite di Dante, Petrarca et Boccaccio*, ed. A. Solerti, Milan, n. d., pp. 292f.). For Bruni, the learning of
Petrarch is not universal and does not include philosophy. In his early letter
to Antonio da S. Miniato, Ficino proposes to abandon his previous rhetorical
style and to speak instead as a philosopher ("deinceps philosophorum more

loquamur verba ubique contempnentes et gravissimas in medium sententias adducentes," Forlì, Biblioteca Communale, Autografo Piancastelli n. 907, see *Studies,* p. 146). In the preface of his *De regimine sanitatis,* Antonio Benivieni relates that he turned from "oratorie artis studia" to philosophy and medicine (ed. L. Belloni, Turin, 1951, p. 19). Alamanno Rinuccini, in the letter to his son Filippo which is a tract on education, insists that it is necessary to proceed from the study of grammar and rhetoric ("ubi nostrorum hominum plerique gradum sistere consueverunt") to that of philosophy (*Lettere ed Orazioni,* ed. Vito R. Giustiniani, Florence, 1953, p. 97). Pontanus in his dialogue *Aegidius* speaks of the decline of eloquence after the end of the Roman Empire, "cum tamen disciplinae ipsae in honore essent habitae, id quod physicorum theologorumque multitudo quae post Boetium extitit plane declarat, tum in Hispania, tum in Gallii Britaniisque ipsaque in Germania" (*I dialoghi,* ed. C. Previtera, Florence, 1943, p. 259).

61. Rossi (*op. cit.,* 6 and 15) cites a poem of Ariosto (1523) for the earliest appearance of the term *umanista* in Italian, and an epigram of the late fifteenth century for the earliest appearance of the term *humanista* in Latin. I have not been able to verify the latter passage, but I found the following passage in a vernacular letter written in 1490 by the rector of Pisa university to the officials in Florence: "avendo le S. V. condocto quello Humanista che non è venuto," this will be a disappointment for many foreign students who have come "per udir̃e humanità" (Angelus Fabronius, *Historia Academiae Pisanae,* I, Pisa, 1791, pp. 369f.). The original letter (Archivio di Stato, Florence, *Studio Fiorentino e Pisano,* XI, f. 14) was sent by Andreas dal Campo notarius studii to the Officiali dello Studio on Dec. 4, 1490. The original has "non essendo venuto" and some other variants not relevant to our problem. During the sixteenth century, the Latin term *humanista* appears in the university documents of Bologna and Ferrara. John Florio in his Italian-English dictionary has the following entry: "Humanista, a humanist or professor of humanitie" (*A Worlde of Wordes,* London, 1598, 164). Other examples of this usage are given by A. Campana ("The Origin of the Word 'Humanist,'" *Journal of the Warburg and Courtauld Institutes,* IX, 1946, 60–73) who arrives at the same conclusion as to the origin and meaning of the term. The term occurs repeatedly in the *Epistolae obscurorum virorum* (K. Brandi, *Das Werden der Renaissance,* Goettingen, 1908, p. 23). The original meaning was still alive in the eighteenth century. S. Salvini (*Fasti Consolari dell'Accademia Fiorentina,* Florence, 1717, p. XIV) mentions Francesco da Buti as a "dottore in grammatica, come allora si dicevano gli Umanisti." And Leibniz states of Valla "qu'il n'étoit pas moins Philosophe, qu' Humaniste" (*Essais de Théodicée,* §405). As a Spanish example of the late sixteenth or early seventeenth century, I noted the following title: "Discurso de las letras humanas llamado el humanista, compuesto por el maestro Francisco Cespedes, Cathedratico de prima de Rethorica en la Universidad de Salamanca" (P. Roca, *Catálogo de los manuscritos que pertenecierón a D. Pascual de Gayangos existentes hoy en la Biblioteca Nacional,* Madrid, 1904, p. 227 n. 643; this is now cod. 17736, as I was informed by Sr. Ramon Paz).

61a. Apparently the term *Humanismus* was coined in 1808 by F. J. Niethammer to denote the educational theory that tried to defend the traditional place of classical studies in the school curriculum (W. Rüegg, *Cicero und der Humanismus,* Zuerich, 1946, pp. 2ff.). Goethe (*Dichtung und Wahrheit,* Bk. XIII, published 1814) uses the term in the sense of humanitarianism (my attention was called to this passage by Prof. Dino Bigongiari).

62. For the relation between theology, medicine, and philosophy in Italy, see H. Rashdall, *The Universities of Europe in the Middle Ages,* 2nd ed. by F. M. Powicke and A. B. Emden, Oxford, 1936, I, 261ff. There is some Aristotelianism in the writings of Urso of Salerno (early thirteenth century), and there was a group of theologians and canonists at Bologna in the twelfth century who were influenced by Abelard. Yet the regular connection between medicine and Aristotelian philosophy, which was to become characteristic of Italian science, appears for the first time in the writings of Taddeo of Florence (late thirteenth century). See now B. Nardi, "L'averroismo bolognese nel secolo XIII e Taddeo Alderotto," *Rivista di Storia della Filosofia,* IV, 1949, 11–22.

63. The influence of the school of Paris upon the earliest Italian Aristotelians ought to be further investigated. The earliest tangible fact seems to be the notice that Gentile da Cingoli, who became a teacher of logic and philosophy at Bologna around 1300, attended a course on Aristotle by Johannes Vate who appears at Paris around 1290 (M. Grabmann, *Mittelalterliches Geistesleben,* II, Munich, 1936, pp. 265f.). It is well known that Peter of Abano, the supposed founder of the school of Padua, studied at Paris and was in personal relations with Jean de Jandun. As late as 1340 the physician Gentile da Foligno is reported to have advised the ruler of Padua to send twelve youths to Paris to study the arts and medicine (H. Denifle and E. Chatelain, *Chartularium Universitatis Parisiensis,* II, Paris, 1891, p. 558).

64. M. Grabmann, "Studien über den Averroisten Taddeo da Parma," *op. cit.* 239–60; Id., "Der Bologneser Averroist Angelo d'Arezzo," *ibid.,* pp. 261–71. Peter of Abano and Gentile da Cingoli belong to the same period. Urbano of Bologna would seem to belong to the second half of the fourteenth century. Anneliese Maier, "Eine italienische Averroistenschule aus der ersten Haelfte des 14. Jahrhunderts," in her *Die Vorlaeufer Galileis im 14. Jahrhundert,* Rome, 1949, pp. 251–78; M. Grabmann, "Gentile da Cingoli, ein italienischer Aristoteleserklaerer aus der Zeit Dantes," *Sitzungsberichte der Bayerischen Akademie der Wissenschaften, Philosophisch-Historische Abteilung,* Jahrgang 1940, Heft 9 (published 1941).

65. P. Duhem, "La tradition de Buridan et la science italienne au XVIe siècle," in his *Études sur Léonard de Vinci,* III, Paris, 1913, pp. 113–259; Id., "La dialectique d'Oxford et la scolastique italienne," *Bulletin Italien,* XII, 1912, and XIII, 1913.

66. For this Italian Aristotelianism, see Ueberweg, *op. cit.,* pp. 22ff. J. Brucker, *Historia critica philosophiae,* IV, pt. I (Leipzig, 1743), 148ff. K. Prantl, *Geschichte der Logik im Abendlande,* IV, Leipzig, 1870, pp. 118ff.; pp. 176ff.; pp. 232ff. E. Renan, *Averroès et l'averroïsme,* Paris, 1852, 2nd rev. ed., Paris, 1861. M. Clagett, *Giovanni Marliani and late Medieval Physics,* New York, 1941; E. Garin, *La filosofia,* Milan, 1947, vol. I, 338–52; II, 1–65. B. Nardi, *Sigieri di Brabante nel pensiero del Rinascimento italiano,* Rome, 1945.

67. Usually the introduction of English dialectic in Italy is attributed to Paul of Venice at Padua about 1400. Yet Peter of Mantua, whom Prantl and Duhem treat as an author of the fifteenth century because of the publica-

tion date of his treatises, lived during the fourteenth century and probably died in 1400 A.D. He taught at Bologna and may have been the first Italian follower of the Oxford school. See the letter addressed to him by Salutati (note 13 above), and Novati's footnote which gives several biographical data and references to manuscripts, all unknown to historians of philosophy. A manuscript with logical works of Peter is at Columbia University Library. The text of the "loyca Ferebrigh" appears in the library of the Franciscans in Assisi as early as 1381 (Manacorda, *op. cit.*, pt. II, p. 361). However, it is known that Peter of Mantua studied at Padua before beginning to teach at Bologna in 1492. See R. Cessi, *Athenaeum* I (Pavia, 1913), 130–131; A. Segarizzi, *Atti della I. R. Accademia di Scienze Lettere ed Arti degli Agiati in Rovereto*, Ser. III, vol. XIII (1907), 219–248.

68. After having joked about the Barbaric names of the English logicians, Bruni continues: "Et quid Colucci ut haec ioca omittam quid est inquam in dialectica quod non Britannicis sophismatibus conturbatum sit?" (*Leonardi Bruni Aretini Dialogus de tribus vatibus Florentinis*, ed. K. Wotke, Vienna, 1889, p. 16).

69. For some of the humanist controversies see R. Sabbadini, *Storia del ciceronianismo*.

70. For Stoic elements in Pomponazzi, see L. Zanta, *La renaissance du Stoicisme au XVIᵉ siècle*, Paris, 1914. For Platonic elements in Pomponazzi see below, art. 6.

71. E. Renan, *Averroès et l'averroïsme*, 2nd ed., Paris, 1861. Renan's work has been superseded for the thirteenth century by P. Mandonnet (*Siger de Brabant et l'averroisme latin au XIIIᵉ siècle*, 2nd ed., 2 vols., Louvain, 1908–11). There is a widespread belief that Renan has been entirely superseded by Mandonnet, but this is obviously not true for the fourteenth and later centuries. The recent article by M. M. Gorce, "Averroisme," *Dictionnaire d'Histoire et de Géographie Ecclésiastique*, V, 1931, 1032–92, does not supersede Renan either, although it supplements him in a few details; Gorce largely follows Renan for the later period and does not correct any of his major mistakes. There is a fairly large literature on Pomponazzi, and a monograph on Cesare Cremonini by L. Mabilleau, *Étude historique sur la philosophie de la Renaissance en Italie*, Paris, 1881. See now Nardi, *op. cit.*

72. An important contribution to the latter problem has been published by J. H. Randall Jr. ("The Development of Scientific Method in the School of Padua," *Journal of the History of Ideas*, I, 1940, 177–206).

73. For the contributions of the Aristotelians to sixteenth-century science, see L. Thorndike, *A History of Magic and Experimental Science*, vols. V-VI, New York, 1941. For Galilei's connection with Italian Aristotelianism, see Randall, *loc. cit.* I should like to add the following detail: Everybody knows Galilei's statement that the nobility of a science depends on the certainty of its method rather than on the dignity of its subject matter (*Opere*, Edizione Nazionale, VI, 1896, p. 237; VII, 1897, p. 246). Remembering this statement, I was surprised to find among Pomponazzi's Questions on the first book of Aristotle's *de anima* the following one: "Nobilitas scientiae a quo sumatur. Quaestio est a quo sumatur magis nobilitas scientiae, an a nobilitate subiecti an a certitudine demonstrationis vel aequaliter ab ambobus" (L. Ferri, "Intorno alle dottrine psicologiche di Pietro Pomponazzi," *Atti della Reale Accademia dei Lincei*, Ser. II, vol. III, 1875–76, pt. III, p. 423). Pomponazzi

does not give a clear answer as does Galilei, but it is obvious that Galilei's statement is not an isolated aphorism, but a conscious answer given to a traditional question debated in the Aristotelian schools of philosophy. See E. Garin, *La Disputa della Arti nel Quattrocento,* Florence, 1947, pp. XIIIff.

74. Most of these notions go back to Renan and have been repeated ever since, especially by French scholars. As I hope to show in a forthcoming study, there is no evidence for the existence of an Alexandrist school in the sixteenth century; there is hardly a uniform Averroist tradition, especially not in the sense used by Renan, who fails to distinguish between the use made of Averroes as a commentator and the adherence to specific Averroist doctrines such as the unity of the intellect; there was no distinctive school of Padua, especially not in the fourteenth century, but merely a broad movement of Italian Aristotelianism in which the university of Padua came to play a leading role during the sixteenth century; many philosophers listed by Renan as representatives of the Paduan school actually never lived in that city; the tradition that the Paduan Aristotelians were atheists and freethinkers is mainly based on unverified anecdotes and insinuations and developed in France during the seventeenth and eighteenth centuries when the freethinkers of that period were looking for forerunners whereas their orthodox opponents had no reason to defend the memory of thinkers who had tried to compromise between reason and faith in a way that was no longer considered permissible or possible by either side. P. O. Kristeller, "Petrarch's 'Averroists,'" *Bibliothèque d'Humanisme et Renaissance* XIV (*Mélanges Augustin Renaudet*) 1952, 59–65. Id., "El Mito del Ateismo Renacentista y la tradición francesa del librepensamiento," *Notas y Estudios de Filosofia* IV 13 (1953) 1–14.

75. On the question of Latin and *volgare* as discussed by the humanists, see R. Sabbadini, *Storia del ciceronianismo,* 127–36. I do not agree with his presentation of the problem. The orations of Romolo Amaseo, and the similar one of Sigonius, were primarily defenses of Latin as a field of study, without any intention to abolish the *volgare.* We still need a history of the Italian literary language that would show its gradual expansion, at the expense of Latin and also of local dialects, according to the various regions of Italy as well as to the various branches of literary expression. The problem was formulated by Burckhardt (13th ed., p. 418). See *Studies,* 473–493.

75a. P. O. Kristeller, "The Modern System of the Arts," *Journal of the History of Ideas* XII 1951, 496 527; XIII 1952, 17–46.

6. THE PHILOSOPHY OF MAN IN THE ITALIAN RENAISSANCE

This lecture was delivered before the Friends of Italy in New York on April 10, 1946.

1. Francesco Petrarca, *Le Familiari,* ed. V. Rossi, vol. I, Florence, 1933, p. 159; cf. Augustine, *Confessions,* x, 8, and Seneca, *Epistles,* 8, 5. The passage of Seneca, not indicated in Rossi's edition, was identified also by G. A. Levi, "Pensiero classico e pensiero cristiano nel Petrarca," *Atene e Roma,* XXXIX, 1937, 77–101, esp. p. 86. See also A. Bobbio, "Seneca e la

formazione spirituale e culturale del Petrarca," *La Bibliofilia,* XLIII, 1941, 224–91. I am indebted for these references to Prof. Dayton Phillips.

2. *De dignitate et excellentia hominis.* I am indebted to Prof. Hans Baron for making available to me his transcription of this rare text.

3. L. Olschki, *Machiavelli the Scientist,* Berkeley, Cal., 1945.

4. *Discorsi,* III, 43.

5. *Opera Omnia,* Basel, 1576, I, p. 944.

6. *Opera Omnia,* Basel, 1572 pp. 351–358. Q. Breen, "Giovanni Pico della Mirandola on the Conflict of Philosophy and Rhetoric," *Journal of the History of Ideas* XIII (1952) 384–426.

6a. See Kristeller, *Studies* (1956), 99–122.

7. *Opera,* p. 131.

8. G. Pico della Mirandola, *De Hominis Dignitate, Heptaplus, De Ente et Uno, e Scritti Vari,* ed. E. Garin, Florence, 1942, pp. 104–106. The English translation is taken from that of Charles Glenn Wallis, *View,* Fall 1944, p. 88f. Another translation by Elizabeth K. Forbes is found in the *Journal of the History of Ideas,* III, 1942, p. 348. See now: *The Renaissance Philosophy of Man,* ed. E. Cassirer, P. O. Kristeller and J. H. Randall Jr., Chicago 1948, 223–54. Variants of the text from ms. Pal. 885 of the Biblioteca Nazionale in Florence have recently been published by E. Garin, "Notizie intorno a Giovanni Pico," *Rivista di Storia della Filosofia,* IV, 1949, 210–12. Ioannes Picus Mirandulanus, *Oratio de hominis dignitate* (Lat. and Engl.), Lexington, Kentucky, 1953.

9. *Opera,* p. 1754.

10. *Opera,* p. 885.

11. *Supplementum Ficinianum,* ed. P. O. Kristeller, Florence, 1937, I, pp. 10f.

12. *Opera,* p. 634. Kristeller, *The Philosophy of Marsilio Ficino,* p. 279; *Il pensiero filosofico di Marsilio Ficino,* p. 300.

13. E. Anagnine, *G. Pico della Mirandola,* Bari, 1937.

13a. For the various meanings of *humanitas,* see E. von Jan, "Humanité," *Zeitschrift für französische Sprache und Literatur,* LV, 1932, 1–66. J. Niedermann, *Kultur,* Florence, 1941, pp. 29ff. and 72ff.

14. *Opera,* p. 635.

15. *De Immortalitate Animae,* ed. and tr. William Henry Hay II, Haverford, 1938, ch. 1, pp. 1f., and III. *The Renaissance Philosophy of Man, op. cit.,* p. 282.

16. *l. c.,* ch. 14, p. 49 and XXVIIIf.

17. *ibid.,* pp. 43 and XXIV.

18. *ibid.,* p. 43 and XXV.

19. *ibid.,* p. 45 and XXVI.

INDEX

Abelard 78, 161
Academy of Plato 26, 50
Academy, Platonic, at Florence 59, 60, 69
Accursius, Francis 155
Aegidius of Viterbo 63
Agricola, Rudolphus 17, 154
Alberti, Leone Battista 17, 19
Alcalà, University of 35
Alciato 101, 154
Alcuin 10
Alexander of Aphrodisias 24, 26, 40ff.
Alexandria (in Egypt) 29, 50
Alfanus of Salerno 151
Alfarabi 54
Amaseo, Romolo 163
Ambrogio Traversari 80
Ambrose, St. 76, 81, 151
Ammonius Saccas 51
Anselm 36, 78, 151, 152
Apologists, Christian 75
Apuleius 54
Aquinas, see Thomas, St.
Arabs, influence on Middle Ages 7; Platonism in 53f.; studies of Aristotle and other Greek authors 27ff.; use of Arabic sources in western Europe 30f., 60, 62
Aretino, Leonardo Bruni 156
Argyropoulos 158
Ariosto 94, 160
Aristotle 7, 11, 12, 16, 17, 21, 24ff. (chapter 2 *passim*), 50ff., 53, 67; influence of, chapter 2; Latin translations of 29-30, 39; nature and transmission of writings 25ff.
Aristotelian tradition and philosophy 12, 22, 24ff. (chapter 2), 56-7, 58, 60, 64, 67-8, 71, 72, 77-8, 82, 120, 161; attacks on 42ff., 58, 64, 67, 85; changes of 38ff.; combined with or adapted to Platonism 26f., 50ff.,

61f.; in the Italian Renaissance 112, 113 *passim,* 126ff.; in medieval curriculum 31ff.; overthrow of in seventeenth century 44ff.
Arnobius 76
Augustine, St. 29, 55, 76, 77, 81, 82, 125, 151, 163; Augustinianism 55ff. *passim;* "Renaissance Augustinianism" 82ff.
Averroes 28-9, 31, 33, 40, 54, 132; Averroism 32f., 37-8, 41, 59, 115; doctrine of the unity of the intellect 33, 37, 63; "Paduan Averroism" 37
Avicebron (Ibn Gabirol) 54, 56
Avicenna 28, 31, 45, 132

Bacon, Francis 35, 68
Baronius 82
Barbaro, Ermolao 40, 43f., 127, 154
Barbaro, Francesco 17
Barzizza 158
Basil 80
Battle of Ancients and Moderns 88
Bayle 22
Bec, school of 78
Bembo 64
Benivieni 63, 159, 160
Berkeley 69
Bernard, St., of Clairvaux 78, 84
Beroaldus, Philippus 154
Bessarion 53, 57, 85
Bible, and Biblical studies in humanist movement 75ff. *passim*
Bobbio, A. 152, 163
Boccaccio 95, 102, 152
Boethius 14, 21, 29f., 54, 56
Bologna, University 36
Bonaventura, St. 36, 78, 151
Boncompagno of Signa 156, 158
Botticelli 65
Bouelles, Charles de 63
Boyle 68

69 70 71 72 73   12 11 10 9 8

Revised December, 1967

hARpER ⚜ TORChbOOKS

HUMANITIES AND SOCIAL SCIENCES

American Studies: General

American Studies: Colonial

American Studies: From the Revolution to 1860

† The New American Nation Series, edited by Henry Steele Commager and Richard B. Morris.
‡ American Perspectives series, edited by Bernard Wishy and William E. Leuchtenburg.
* The Rise of Modern Europe series, edited by William L. Langer.
** History of Europe series, edited by J. H. Plumb.
¶ Researches in the Social, Cultural and Behavioral Sciences, edited by Benjamin Nelson.
§ The Library of Religion and Culture, edited by Benjamin Nelson.
Σ Harper Modern Science Series, edited by James R. Newman.
° Not for sale in Canada.
△ Not for sale in the U. K.

1

2

L. S. B. LEAKEY: Adam's Ancestors: *The Evolution of Man and His Culture.* △ Illus.   TB/1019
EDWARD BURNETT TYLOR: Religion in Primitive Culture. Part II of "Primitive Culture." § Intro. by Paul Radin
                                                                                    TB/34
W. LLOYD WARNER: A Black Civilization: *A Study of an Australian Tribe.* ¶ Illus.   TB/3056

Art and Art History

WALTER LOWRIE: Art in the Early Church. *Revised Edition.* 452 illus.   TB/124
EMILE MÂLE: The Gothic Image: *Religious Art in France of the Thirteenth Century.* § △ 190 illus.   TB/44
MILLARD MEISS: Painting in Florence and Siena after the Black Death: *The Arts, Religion and Society in the Mid-Fourteenth Century.* 169 illus.   TB/1148
ERICH NEUMANN: The Archetypal World of Henry Moore. △ 107 illus.   TB/2020
DORA & ERWIN PANOFSKY: Pandora's Box: *The Changing Aspects of a Mythical Symbol. Revised Edition. Illus.*
                                                                                    TB/2021
ERWIN PANOFSKY: Studies in Iconology: *Humanistic Themes in the Art of the Renaissance.* △ 180 illustrations   TB/1077
ALEXANDRE PIANKOFF: The Shrines of Tut-Ankh-Amon. *Edited by N. Rambova.* 117 illus.   TB/2011
JEAN SEZNEC: The Survival of the Pagan Gods: *The Mythological Tradition and Its Place in Renaissance Humanism and Art.* 108 illustrations   TB/2004
OTTO VON SIMSON: The Gothic Cathedral: *Origins of Gothic Architecture and the Medieval Concept of Order.* △ 58 illus.   TB/2018
HEINRICH ZIMMER: Myth and Symbols in Indian Art and Civilization. 70 illustrations   TB/2005

Business, Economics & Economic History

REINHARD BENDIX: Work and Authority in Industry: *Ideologies of Management in the Course of Industrialization*   TB/3035
GILBERT BURCK & EDITORS OF FORTUNE: The Computer Age: *And Its Potential for Management*   TB/1179
THOMAS C. COCHRAN: The American Business System: *A Historical Perspective, 1900-1955* TB/1080
THOMAS C. COCHRAN: The Inner Revolution: *Essays on the Social Sciences in History* △   TB/1140
THOMAS C. COCHRAN & WILLIAM MILLER: The Age of Enterprise: *A Social History of Industrial America* TB/1054
ROBERT DAHL & CHARLES E. LINDBLOM: Politics, Economics, and Welfare: *Planning and Politico-Economic Systems Resolved into Basic Social Processes*
                                                                                    TB/3037
PETER F. DRUCKER: The New Society: *The Anatomy of Industrial Order* △   TB/1082
EDITORS OF FORTUNE: America in the Sixties: *The Economy and the Society*   TB/1015
ROBERT L. HEILBRONER: The Great Ascent: *The Struggle for Economic Development in Our Time* TB/3030
ROBERT L. HEILBRONER: The Limits of American Capitalism   TB/1305
FRANK H. KNIGHT: The Economic Organization TB/1214
FRANK H. KNIGHT: Risk, Uncertainty and Profit TB/1215
ABBA P. LERNER: Everybody's Business: *Current Assumptions in Economics and Public Policy* TB/3051
ROBERT GREEN MC CLOSKEY: American Conservatism in the Age of Enterprise, 1865-1910 △   TB/1137
PAUL MANTOUX: The Industrial Revolution in the Eighteenth Century: *The Beginnings of the Modern Factory System in England* ○ △   TB/1079
WILLIAM MILLER, Ed.: Men in Business: *Essays on the Historical Role of the Entrepreneur*   TB/1081
RICHARD B. MORRIS: Government and Labor in Early America △   TB/1244

HERBERT SIMON: The Shape of Automation: *For Men and Management*   TB/1245
PERRIN STRYKER: The Character of the Executive: *Eleven Studies in Managerial Qualities*   TB/1041

Education

JACQUES BARZUN: The House of Intellect △   TB/1051
RICHARD M. JONES, Ed.: Contemporary Educational Psychology: *Selected Readings*   TB/1292
CLARK KERR: The Uses of the University   TB/1264
JOHN U. NEF: Cultural Foundations of Industrial Civilization △   TB/1024

Historiography & Philosophy of History

JACOB BURCKHARDT: On History and Historians. △ *Introduction by H. R. Trevor-Roper*   TB/1216
WILHELM DILTHEY: Pattern and Meaning in History: *Thoughts on History and Society.* ○ △ *Edited with an Introduction by H. P. Rickman*   TB/1075
J. H. HEXTER: Reappraisals in History: *New Views on History & Society in Early Modern Europe* △ TB/1100
H. STUART HUGHES: History as Art and as Science: *Twin Vistas on the Past*   TB/1207
RAYMOND KLIBANSKY & H. J. PATON, Eds.: Philosophy and History: *The Ernst Cassirer Festschrift. Illus.*
                                                                                    TB/1115
ARNALDO MOMIGLIANO: Studies in Historiography ○ △
                                                                                    TB/1283
GEORGE H. NADEL, Ed.: Studies in the Philosophy of History: *Selected Essays from History and Theory*
                                                                                    TB/1208
JOSE ORTEGA Y GASSET: The Modern Theme. *Introduction by Jose Ferrater Mora*   TB/1038
KARL R. POPPER: The Open Society and Its Enemies △
   Vol. I: *The Spell of Plato*   TB/1101
   Vol. II: *The High Tide of Prophecy: Hegel, Marx and the Aftermath*   TB/1102
KARL R. POPPER: The Poverty of Historicism ○ △ TB/1126
G. J. RENIER: History: Its Purpose and Method △ TB/1209
W. H. WALSH: Philosophy of History: *An Introduction* △
                                                                                    TB/1020

History: General

WOLFGANG FRANKE: China and the West. *Trans by R. A. Wilson*   TB/1326
L. CARRINGTON GOODRICH: A Short History of the Chinese People. △ Illus.   TB/3015
DAN N. JACOBS & HANS H. BAERWALD: Chinese Communism: *Selected Documents*   TB/3031
BERNARD LEWIS: The Arabs in History △   TB/1029
BERNARD LEWIS: The Middle East and the West ○ △
                                                                                    TB/1274

History: Ancient

A. ANDREWES: The Greek Tyrants △   TB/1103
ADOLF ERMAN, Ed. The Ancient Egyptians: *A Sourcebook of Their Writings. New material and Introduction by William Kelly Simpson*   TB/1233
MICHAEL GRANT: Ancient History ○ △   TB/1190
SAMUEL NOAH KRAMER: Sumerian Mythology   TB/1055
NAPHTALI LEWIS & MEYER REINHOLD, Eds.: Roman Civilization. *Sourcebook I: The Republic*   TB/1231
NAPHTALI LEWIS & MEYER REINHOLD, Eds.: Roman Civilization. *Sourcebook II: The Empire*   TB/1232

History: Medieval

P. BOISSONNADE: Life and Work in Medieval Europe: *The Evolution of the Medieval Economy, the 5th to the 15th Century.* ○ △ *Preface by Lynn White, Jr.* TB/1141
HELEN CAM: England before Elizabeth △   TB/1026
NORMAN COHN: The Pursuit of the Millennium: *Revolutionary Messianism in Medieval and Reformation Europe* △   TB/1037

VESPASIANO: Renaissance Princes, Popes, and Prelates: *The Vespasiano Memoirs: Lives of Illustrious Men of the XVth Century.* Intro. by Myron P. Gilmore TB/1111

History: Modern European

FREDERICK B. ARTZ: Reaction and Revolution, 1815-1832. * *Illus.* TB/3034
MAX BELOFF: The Age of Absolutism, 1660-1815 △ TB/1062
ROBERT C. BINKLEY: Realism and Nationalism, 1852-1871. * *Illus.* TB/3038
EUGENE C. BLACK, Ed.: European Political History, 1815-1870: *Aspects of Liberalism* TB/1331
ASA BRIGGS: The Making of Modern England, 1784-1867: *The Age of Improvement* ° △ TB/1203
CRANE BRINTON: A Decade of Revolution, 1789-1799. * *Illus.* TB/3018
D. W. BROGAN: The Development of Modern France. ° △
Volume I: *From the Fall of the Empire to the Dreyfus Affair* TB/1184
Volume II: *The Shadow of War, World War I, Between the Two Wars. New Introduction by the Author* TB/1185
J. BRONOWSKI & BRUCE MAZLISH: The Western Intellectual Tradition: *From Leonardo to Hegel* △ TB/3001
GEOFFREY BRUUN: Europe and the French Imperium, 1799-1814. * *Illus.* TB/3033
ALAN BULLOCK: Hitler, A Study in Tyranny. ° △ *Illus.* TB/1123
E. H. CARR: German-Soviet Relations Between the Two World Wars, 1919-1939 TB/1278
E. H. CARR: International Relations Between the Two World Wars, 1919-1939 ° △ TB/1279
E. H. CARR: The Twenty Years' Crisis, 1919-1939: *An Introduction to the Study of International Relations* ° △ TB/1122
GORDON A. CRAIG: From Bismarck to Adenauer: *Aspects of German Statecraft. Revised Edition* TB/1171
DENIS DIDEROT: The Encyclopedia: *Selections. Ed. and trans. by Stephen Gendzier* TB/1299
WALTER L. DORN: Competition for Empire, 1740-1763. * *Illus.* TB/3032
FRANKLIN L. FORD: Robe and Sword: *The Regrouping of the French Aristocracy after Louis XIV* TB/1217
CARL J. FRIEDRICH: The Age of the Baroque, 1610-1660. * *Illus.* TB/3004
RENÉ FUELOEP-MILLER: The Mind and Face of Bolshevism: *An Examination of Cultural Life in Soviet Russia. New Epilogue by the Author* TB/1188
M. DOROTHY GEORGE: London Life in the Eighteenth Century △ TB/1182
LEO GERSHOY: From Despotism to Revolution, 1763-1789. * *Illus.* TB/3017
C. C. GILLISPIE: Genesis and Geology: *The Decades before Darwin* § TB/51
ALBERT GOODWIN, Ed.: The European Nobility in the Eighteenth Century △ TB/1313
ALBERT GOODWIN: The French Revolution △ TB/1064
ALBERT GUÉRARD: France in the Classical Age: *The Life and Death of an Ideal* △ TB/1183
CARLTON J. H. HAYES: A Generation of Materialism, 1871-1900. * *Illus.* TB/3039
J. H. HEXTER: Reappraisals in History: *New Views on History and Society in Early Modern Europe* △ TB/1100
STANLEY HOFFMANN et al.: In Search of France: *The Economy, Society and Political System in the Twentieth Century* TB/1219
A. R. HUMPHREYS: The Augustan World: *Society, Thought, & Letters in 18th Century England* ° △ TB/1105
DAN N. JACOBS, Ed.: The New Communist Manifesto and Related Documents. *Third edition, revised* TB/1078

LIONEL KOCHAN: The Struggle for Germany: *1914-45* TB/1304
HANS KOHN: The Mind of Germany: *The Education of a Nation* △ TB/1204
HANS KOHN, Ed.: The Mind of Modern Russia: *Historical and Political Thought of Russia's Great Age* TB/1065
WALTER LAQUEUR & GEORGE L. MOSSE, Eds.: Education and Social Structure in the 20th Century. ° △ *Vol. 6 of the Journal of Contemporary History* TB/1339
WALTER LAQUEUR & GEORGE L. MOSSE, Eds.: International Fascism, 1920-1945. ° △ *Volume 1 of Journal of Contemporary History* TB/1276
WALTER LAQUEUR & GEORGE L. MOSSE, Eds.: The Left-Wing Intellectuals between the Wars 1919-1939. ° △ *Volume 2 of Journal of Contemporary History* TB/1286
WALTER LAQUEUR & GEORGE L. MOSSE, Eds.: Literature and Politics in the 20th Century. ° △ *Vol. 5 of the Journal of Contemporary History* TB/1328
WALTER LAQUEUR & GEORGE L. MOSSE, Eds.: The New History: *Trends in Historical Research and Writing since World War II.* ° △ *Vol. 4 of the Journal of Contemporary History* TB/1327
WALTER LAQUEUR & GEORGE L. MOSSE, Eds.: 1914: *The Coming of the First World War.* ° △ *Volume 3 of Journal of Contemporary History* TB/1306
FRANK E. MANUEL: The Prophets of Paris: *Turgot, Condorcet, Saint-Simon, Fourier, and Comte* TB/1218
KINGSLEY MARTIN: French Liberal Thought in the Eighteenth Century: *A Study of Political Ideas from Bayle to Condorcet* TB/1114
ROBERT K. MERTON: Science, Technology and Society in Seventeenth Century England ¶ *New Intro. by the Author* TB/1324
L. B. NAMIER: Facing East: *Essays on Germany, the Balkans, and Russia in the 20th Century* △ TB/1280
L. B. NAMIER: Personalities and Powers: *Selected Essays* △ TB/1186
L. B. NAMIER: Vanished Supremacies: *Essays on European History, 1812-1918* ° TB/1088
NAPOLEON III: Napoleonic Ideas: *Des Idées Napoléoniennes, par le Prince Napoléon-Louis Bonaparte. Ed. by Brison D. Gooch* TB/1336
FRANZ NEUMANN: Behemoth: *The Structure and Practice of National Socialism, 1933-1944* TB/1289
FREDERICK L. NUSSBAUM: The Triumph of Science and Reason, 1660-1685. * *Illus.* TB/3009
DAVID OGG: Europe of the Ancien Régime, 1715-1783 ** ° △ TB/1271
JOHN PLAMENATZ: German Marxism and Russian Communism. ° △ *New Preface by the Author* TB/1189
RAYMOND W. POSTGATE, Ed.: Revolution from 1789 to 1906: *Selected Documents* TB/1063
PENFIELD ROBERTS: The Quest for Security, 1715-1740. * *Illus.* TB/3016
PRISCILLA ROBERTSON: Revolutions of 1848: *A Social History* TB/1025
GEORGE RUDÉ: Revolutionary Europe, 1783-1815 ** ° △ TB/1272
LOUIS, DUC DE SAINT-SIMON: Versailles, The Court, and Louis XIV. ° △ *Introductory Note by Peter Gay* TB/1250
HUGH SETON-WATSON: Eastern Europe Between the Wars, 1918-1941 TB/1330
ALBERT SOREL: Europe Under the Old Regime. *Translated by Francis H. Herrick* TB/1121
N. N. SUKHANOV: The Russian Revolution, 1917: *Eyewitness Account.* △ *Edited by Joel Carmichael*
Vol. I TB/1066; Vol. II TB/1067
A. J. P. TAYLOR: From Napoleon to Lenin: *Historical Essays* ° △ TB/1268
A. J. P. TAYLOR: The Habsburg Monarchy, 1809-1918: *A History of the Austrian Empire and Austria-Hungary* ° △ TB/1187
G. M. TREVELYAN: British History in the Nineteenth Century and After: 1782-1919. ° △ *Second Edition* TB/1251

5

HANS KOHN: Political Ideologies of the 20th Century
TB/1277
ROY C. MACRIDIS, Ed.: Political Parties: *Contemporary Trends and Ideas* TB/1322
ROBERT GREEN MC CLOSKEY: American Conservatism in the Age of Enterprise, 1865-1910 TB/1137
KINGSLEY MARTIN: French Liberal Thought in the Eighteenth Century: *Political Ideas from Bayle to Condorcet* △ TB/1114
ROBERTO MICHELS: First Lectures in Political Sociology. *Edited by Alfred de Grazia* ¶ ° TB/1224
JOHN STUART MILL: On Bentham and Coleridge. △ *Introduction by F. R. Leavis* TB/1070
BARRINGTON MOORE, JR.: Political Power and Social Theory: *Seven Studies* ¶ TB/1221
BARRINGTON MOORE, JR.: Soviet Politics—The Dilemma of Power: *The Role of Ideas in Social Change* ¶
TB/1222
BARRINGTON MOORE, JR.: Terror and Progress—USSR: *Some Sources of Change and Stability in the Soviet Dictatorship* ¶ TB/1266
JOHN B. MORRALL: Political Thought in Medieval Times △ TB/1076
JOHN PLAMENATZ: German Marxism and Russian Communism. ° △ *New Preface by the Author* TB/1189
KARL R. POPPER: The Open Society and Its Enemies △
Vol. I: *The Spell of Plato* TB/1101
Vol. II: *The High Tide of Prophecy: Hegel, Marx and the Aftermath* TB/1102
JOHN P. ROCHE, Ed.: American Political Thought: *From Jefferson to Progressivism* TB/1332
HENRI DE SAINT-SIMON: Social Organization, The Science of Man, and Other Writings. *Edited and Translated by Felix Markham* TB/1152
CHARLES I. SCHOTTLAND, Ed.: The Welfare State TB/1323
JOSEPH A. SCHUMPETER: Capitalism, Socialism and Democracy △ TB/3008
BENJAMIN I. SCHWARTZ: Chinese Communism and the Rise of Mao TB/1308
CHARLES H. SHINN: Mining Camps: *A Study in American Frontier Government.* ‡ *Edited by Rodman W. Paul*
TB/3062
PETER WOLL, Ed.: Public Administration and Policy: *Selected Essays* TB/1284

Psychology

ALFRED ADLER: The Individual Psychology of Alfred Adler. △ *Edited by Heinz L. and Rowena R. Ansbacher*
TB/1154
ALFRED ADLER: Problems of Neurosis. *Introduction by Heinz L. Ansbacher* TB/1145
ARTHUR BURTON & ROBERT E. HARRIS, Eds.: Clinical Studies of Personality
Vol. I TB/3075; Vol. II TB/3076
HADLEY CANTRIL: The Invasion from Mars: *A Study in the Psychology of Panic* ¶ TB/1282
HERBERT FINGARETTE: The Self in Transformation: *Psychoanalysis, Philosophy and the Life of the Spirit* ¶
TB/1177
SIGMUND FREUD: On Creativity and the Unconscious: *Papers on the Psychology of Art, Literature, Love, Religion.* § △ *Intro. by Benjamin Nelson* TB/45
C. JUDSON HERRICK: The Evolution of Human Nature
TB/545
WILLIAM JAMES: Psychology: *The Briefer Course. Edited with an Intro. by Gordon Allport* TB/1034
C. G. JUNG: Psychological Reflections △ TB/2001
C. G. JUNG: Symbols of Transformation: *An Analysis of the Prelude to a Case of Schizophrenia.* △ *Illus.*
Vol. I TB/2009; Vol. II TB/2010
C. G. JUNG & C. KERÉNYI: Essays on a Science of Mythology: *The Myths of the Divine Child and the Divine Maiden*

KARL MENNINGER: Theory of Psychoanalytic Technique
TB/1144
ERICH NEUMANN: Amor and Psyche: *The Psychic Development of the Feminine* △ TB/2012
ERICH NEUMANN: The Archetypal World of Henry Moore. △ *107 illus.* TB/2020
ERICH NEUMANN: The Origins and History of Consciousness △ Vol. I *Illus.* TB/2007; Vol. II TB/2008
RALPH BARTON PERRY: The Thought and Character of William James: *Briefer Version* TB/1156
JOHN H. SCHAAR: Escape from Authority: *The Perspectives of Erich Fromm* TB/1155
MUZAFER SHERIF: The Psychology of Social Norms
TB/3072

Sociology

JACQUES BARZUN: Race: *A Study in Superstition. Revised Edition* TB/1172
BERNARD BERELSON, Ed.: The Behavioral Sciences Today
TB/1127
ABRAHAM CAHAN: The Rise of David Levinsky: *A documentary novel of social mobility in early twentieth century America. Intro. by John Higham* TB/1028
KENNETH B. CLARK: Dark Ghetto: *Dilemmas of Social Power. Foreword by Gunnar Myrdal* TB/1317
LEWIS A. COSER, Ed.: Political Sociology TB/1293
ALLISON DAVIS & JOHN DOLLARD: Children of Bondage: *The Personality Development of Negro Youth in the Urban South* ¶ TB/3049
ST. CLAIR DRAKE & HORACE R. CAYTON: Black Metropolis: *A Study of Negro Life in a Northern City.* △ *Revised and Enlarged. Intro. by Everett C. Hughes*
Vol. I TB/1086; Vol. II TB/1087
EMILE DURKHEIM et al.: Essays on Sociology and Philosophy: *With Analyses of Durkheim's Life and Work.* ¶ *Edited by Kurt H. Wolff* TB/1151
LEON FESTINGER, HENRY W. RIECKEN & STANLEY SCHACHTER: When Prophecy Fails: *A Social and Psychological Account of a Modern Group that Predicted the Destruction of the World* ¶ TB/1132
ALVIN W. GOULDNER: Wildcat Strike: *A Study in Worker-Management Relationships* ¶ TB/1176
CÉSAR GRAÑA: Modernity and Its Discontents: *French Society and the French Man of Letters in the Nineteenth Century* ¶ TB/1318
FRANCIS J. GRUND: Aristocracy in America: *Social Class in the Formative Years of the New Nation* △ TB/1001
KURT LEWIN: Field Theory in Social Science: *Selected Theoretical Papers.* ¶ △ *Edited with a Foreword by Dorwin Cartwright* TB/1135
R. M. MAC IVER: Social Causation TB/1153
ROBERT K. MERTON, LEONARD BROOM, LEONARD S. COTTRELL, JR., Editors: Sociology Today: *Problems and Prospects* ¶ Vol. I TB/1173; Vol. II TB/1174
ROBERTO MICHELS: First Lectures in Political Sociology. *Edited by Alfred de Grazia* ¶ ° TB/1224
BARRINGTON MOORE, JR.: Political Power and Social Theory: *Seven Studies* ¶ TB/1221
BARRINGTON MOORE, JR.: Soviet Politics—The Dilemma of Power: *The Role of Ideas in Social Change* ¶
TB/1222
TALCOTT PARSONS & EDWARD A. SHILS, Editors: Toward a General Theory of Action: *Theoretical Foundations for the Social Sciences* TB/1083
ARNOLD ROSE: The Negro in America: *The Condensed Version of Gunnar Myrdal's An American Dilemma*
TB/3048
GEORGE ROSEN: Madness in Society: *Chapters in the Historical Sociology of Mental Illness.* ¶ *Preface by Benjamin Nelson* TB/1337
KURT SAMUELSSON: Religion and Economic Action: *A Critique of Max Weber's The Protestant Ethic and the Spirit of Capitalism.* ¶ ° *Trans. by E. G. French. Ed. with Intro. by D. C. Coleman* TB/1131

RELIGION

Ancient & Classical

Biblical Thought & Literature

The Judaic Tradition

Christianity: General

Christianity: Origins & Early Development

Oriental Religions: Far Eastern, Near Eastern

Philosophy of Religion

Religion, Culture & Society

NATURAL SCIENCES AND MATHEMATICS

Biological Sciences

Chemistry

Communication Theory

Geography

History of Science

12